MAP

a market anti-inflation plan

D1592578

MAP

a market anti-inflation plan

ABBA P. LERNER
the florida state university

DAVID C. COLANDER
university of miami

HARCOURT BRACE JOVANOVICH, INC.
new york   san diego   chicago   san francisco   atlanta
london   sydney   toronto

To Daliah and Maura
for keeping love and order in our lives

acknowledgments

This book was conceived in Chicago when we met at the 1978 American Economics Association Convention. The first draft was written in December 1978 at Florida State University, to which we are especially indebted. For encouragement, stimulation, and support, we would like to thank Maura Colander, Eldon J. Dvorak, Katharine Jacobson, Daliah Lerner, Edmund Phelps, Larry Seidman, William Vickrey, and Sidney Weintraub.

In working toward the final MAP proposal, we benefited from feedback in lectures and seminars at the Eastern, the Western, the Atlantic, and the American Economic Associations; at the City University of New York, Stanford University, the University of California at Berkeley, Santa Barbara, and Los Angeles, Fullerton State University, Northwestern University, Columbia University, Oxford University, Johns Hopkins University, the University of Miami, and the Federal Reserve Board; and at conferences on inflation at Florida State University, Middlebury College, Tel Aviv University, and the Brookings Institution.

Between December 1978 and November 1979, the book was extensively revised, benefiting from comments by George Bishop, Alfred Gossner, Alfred Kahn, Alice Rivlin, William Vickrey, and Martin Wolf. We must also thank Oxford University, Tel Aviv University, the Bank of Israel, the London School of Economics, the London Business School, and the University of Miami for assistance in the course of the revision.

Finally, we must thank our editor, Mary George, for her painstaking stylistic improvements.

preface

This is a small book about a big topic. This is not the usual book on inflation, simplified—or oversimplified—to make accepted doctrines intelligible to the layman. It presents a new plan—MAP (Market Anti-inflation Plan)—that makes it possible to succeed in curing our inflation. The ideas in it are not easily absorbed. They form a radical new framework—a new way of looking at inflation, and indeed at all macroeconomics, which is at the same time only a synthesis of many divergent old trains of thought. As Albert Einstein said, "Ideas should be expressed as simply as possible, but not more so." We think we have made the book intelligible to nonspecialists, even though its ideas are challenging for all readers, and perhaps even more so for advanced economists.

We approach inflation as an *economic* problem, but we make allowances for political realities in designing MAP. Although we believe MAP should be adopted in some form, the book is not written from an advocatory position. We try to consider all arguments, both pro and con, and do not attempt to minimize potential difficulties.

The methodology is realytic*—an unusual word that indicates a contrast with analytic. This means that we are primarily concerned with solving *real* problems. We believe that the book also contributes importantly to extending theoretical understanding, but it does this only where necessary to solve the problem at hand.

There are fifteen chapters. Chapter 1 introduces and summarizes the MAP concept. Chapters 2–5 present the theory of MAP and the story of its development. Chapter 6 contains the formal MAP framework, and Chapter 7 examines some of the ways the framework can be fleshed out for practical applications. Chapter 8 investigates the problems of starting up MAP. The rest of the book is devoted to clearing up misunderstandings and tying up loose ends—at least those we have anticipated

Abba P. Lerner
David C. Colander

---

*Professor A.C. Pigou (1922) used, perhaps invented, the word "realitic." We have spelled it with a "y" to emphasize its relation to "analytic" and to prevent typists and typesetters from "correcting" it to "realistic."

contents

A claim of a solution to inflation and stagflation (and the natural skepticism). The nature of the problem and the conditions for its solution. The unacceptable cure by monetary and fiscal policy. The infeasible cure by wage and price control. Inflation-pollution. Recent progress in incentive plans. The flaw in our economic system. How MAP can achieve the cure by combining the positive elements in all these approaches with the use of the market mechanism. How this leaves all actual prices and wages free while stabilizing the average price (the price level), enabling monetary-fiscal policy to practice sound finance. MAP's novel device: an anti-inflation credit (MAP Credit), which keeps the increase in total national Net Sales equal to the increase in total national output, thereby preventing price inflation.

The meaning and measure of inflation. Its popularity and unpopularity. Its great importance (although often exaggerated). A "pure" and "harmless" inflation. "Relative price" and the importance of average price stability. The metaphysical search for and the practical discovery of "the cause" of inflation. A flaw in the economic mechanism as the cause and MAP as the cure.

3

the history of anti-inflation policies:
money and the limits to
money management   **14**

The natural history of the development of money and of money management for the regulation of total spending. Problems in the management of the supply of money. How demand inflation turns into expectational inflation. How this turns the classical lessons upside down. Reversed causation or circular causation. A practical dilemma.

4

the history of anti-inflation policies:
controls and incomes policies   **21**

The natural history of the development of the "direct" anti-inflation measures accompanying excess demand, from price controls via black markets, informal and formal rationing, and "general rationing" to suppressed inflation and social disruption. Incomes policy, bureaucratic. Incomes policy, tax-based. Improved "carrot-and-stick" incomes policies. Using the market as well as price. An early "Lerner Plan." The Wage Increase Permit Plan (WIPP). A fatal objection and how it is overcome by MAP.

5

the road to MAP 32

Demand inflation and expectational inflation. Spare capacity. How demand inflation becomes expectational inflation. Why spending restraint and wage–price regulation cannot correct the flaw in the economic system. The incompatibility of price regulation with the market system. Five essential elements in a successful solution to inflation: a counter-inflationary disincentive; its appropriate strength; its automatic adjustment; fairness; and simplicity. How spending policy and controls fail to provide these conditions. Additional benefits from MAP: a guide for sound finance; its neutrality between labor and capital and between public and private enterprise; its self-disinflation as the inflation is reduced; its readiness if needed again; and its reversibility for expectational deflation.

6

the MAP framework 39

A simple variation of MAP. Model A for a quick and complete cure of stagflation. The rules and definitions. What MAP does *not* do. The interdependence of sound finance and price stability. A simplified example of the operation of MAP on the economy as a whole. A simplified example of the operation of MAP on firms with different expectations. The path from a stabilized price level to stabilized expectations. The market price of MAP Credit. The operation of MAP in disinflation and deflation.

7

variants of MAP   50

Use of institutions other than the Federal Reserve System. The "orderly marketing" of MAP Credit. Possible exemptions of parts of the economy from MAP: agriculture, small firms, government, and nonprofit organizations. Should firms or individuals be responsible for MAP Credit adjustments? Alternative ways of measuring Net Sales, factor inputs, investment, and depreciation. Should taxes take the form of lower incomes or higher prices? The problems of new workers and reemployed retirees. Investment in specialized skills. The problems of the timing of auditing. How most problems fade away as the price of MAP Credit approaches zero.

8

the problems of starting up MAP   59

The initial allocation of MAP Credit—administrative versus formula approaches. A sudden or gradual ending of inflation. Starting off the MAP Credit market. The illusions of money illusion. Some effects of a temporary, initially high MAP Credit price.

9

MAP and functional finance   64

Deficits do *not* cause inflation. The analogy with private investment. The constituents of a deficit and their connections with demand inflation. The cause and cure of demand inflation. "Monetarism." How MAP depends on functional finance and how functional finance depends on MAP. How MAP would resolve the debate between monetarism and fiscalism.

10

some technical issues   69

This book's *realytic* methodology. The severe limitations of rigorous mathematical models. MAP Credit as a new commodity with the MAP rules as the required additional equation. In equilibrium, excess demand (for example, for MAP Credit) sums to zero, but not necessarily at a constant price level. A natural range of unemployment. The conditions required to achieve a nonzero price of MAP Credit. Limits to the price of MAP Credit. Possible effects on economic adjustment speeds. How a high price for MAP Credit reduces windfalls and profit dispersions rather than productivity. The effects of expected changes in the price of MAP Credit. Some international aspects.

11

other novel proposals   78

Tax-based Incomes Policies (TIP) can hardly be understood properly without the MAP concept. They are tax analogues to the corresponding market-based incomes policies. A design for an optimal TIP and three reasons why MAP still seems preferable. Indexation as an aid to living with inflation and the claims that indexation could also aid in fighting inflation by reducing government profits from inflation (in contrast to MAP's view that the government is also a victim of inflation). Some other market anti-inflation schemes based on spending per unit of output (MAP is based on spending per unit of input). A final note of von Hayek's and Klein's proposals for a "free market in money supply," the concept of "direct relativity bargaining," and some "scaling down" systems for wages and prices.

12

the government's anti-inflation program 87

Statement of government's position. Points which help, points which are irrelevant to, and points which hinder the proposed solutions to stagflation. Points which are missing but which are supplied by MAP.

13

business' anti-inflation program 100

Statement of business' position. Points which help, points which are irrelevant to, and points which hinder the proposed solutions to stagflation. Points which are missing but which are supplied by MAP.

14

labor's anti-inflation program 107

Statement of labor's position. Points which help, points which are irrelevant to, and points which hinder the proposed solutions to stagflation. Points which are missing but which are supplied by MAP.

15

conclusion   115

How Keynes returned the problem of unemployment to economics by treating it not as a political issue but as a technical problem in the economic system. How Keynesianism was pronounced dead—both by the right and the left—because it could not prevent or cure expectational inflation. How MAP treats expectational inflation as a technical problem, returning it to economics. The role of the government in stopping expectational inflation by first stopping the inflation. Some hopeful signs of possible wide-ranging support for MAP. How MAP's theoretical neatness may be translated into political acceptability as we go through at least one more unnecessary round of eclectic shilly-shallying, another dose of an artificially induced money crunch with severe depression and unemployment, and another administrative nightmare of regulatory wage and price controls. How the simplification, the improvements, and the softening of the controls could lead to the gradual development of a more and more MAP-like incomes policy—even if we do not choose a more direct route to MAP.

MAP

a market anti-inflation plan

1

introduction

If we told you that there is a solution to inflation, you would be skeptical—and rightly so. If we added that the natural economic solution to inflation has been lying under our noses since Adam Smith wrote *The Wealth of Nations,* you would probably decide that we were two wild-eyed academics who had spent too much time cooped up in the ivory tower.

Thus, it is with some trepidation that we write this book, arguing that inflation does have a solution. That solution is the Market Anti-inflation Accounting Plan—or, for short, the Market Anti-inflation Plan (MAP).

a novel combination

Hesitation about the existence of a solution to inflation is well justified by experience with past remedies, no matter what they are called or how they are packaged. But MAP is not simply old wine in a new bottle. Nor is it an entirely new concoction. MAP is only a novel way of distilling and combining the sound elements contained in the old remedies that have failed.

The problems of the old remedies are well known. Sufficiently restrictive monetary policy alone is politically unacceptable, so it can be laid aside without even discussing the other problems it poses. Wage and price controls may once more become politically acceptable, but they are administratively infeasible and provide no satisfactory basis for a solution to inflation. Painful experience has taught us that neither of these methods works.

Still, each of these traditional remedies contains an important element of truth: any solution to inflation must somehow achieve the monetary restrictionists' objective of keeping the growth of total *money* spending parallel with the growth of *real* spending—the real goods purchased. But this parallelism—essential as it is to the maintenance of a stable price level— must be achieved in a way that also satisfies the objective of the advocates of wage and price controls. Thus, the parallelism must be reached at a *satisfactory level of real spending,* not by sacrificing employment and prosperity to achieve a predetermined level of *money* spending.

a plan and a policy

The objectives of *both* the restrictionists and the wage and price advocates can be achieved by the coordination of a *plan* for stabilizing wage and price

1

levels (without turning to controls) with a *policy* of maintaining a satisfactory level of total *real* spending in the economy.

The *plan* must satisfy the following conditions:

(1) It must stabilize the *average* price (the price level).
(2) It must be generally accepted as *fair* by all parties involved in these decisions.
(3) It must arrange for the adjustment of all actual prices and wages to changing tastes, techniques, and availabilities, so that the markets are cleared and there are no continuing gluts or shortages.

The *policy* must be a "functional finance" monetary and fiscal policy of keeping total money spending in the economy sufficient, but not more than sufficient, to maintain "full employment" prosperity at current prices. Although the objective of the *plan* would be to stabilize prices and the objective of the *policy* would be to maintain prosperity, each would *depend* on the other and at the same time would *contribute* to the special responsibility of the other.

why previous plans failed

Attempts to cure our present inflation have failed because they did not satisfy all the necessary conditions. This seems also to be true of the government's present anti-inflation plan and of the other anti-inflation proposals now being considered.

Monetary restraint is politically unacceptable, not so much because it involves the loss of potential output but because it violates condition (2) in that it concentrates a heavy burden on the unemployed minority. There are those who claim that if only excessive monetary expansion had not been permitted in the past, none of our stagflation problems would have arisen. But even if this is true, and even if in some future time a correct monetary policy would completely protect us from these troubles, this does nothing to change the unacceptability of monetary restraint as a solution to our present stagflation problem.

When applied crudely—perhaps only initially—as a freeze on all wages and prices, wage and price controls immediately satisfy condition (1). But they do not satisfy conditions (2) or (3). The controllers then develop guidelines and guideposts, attempting to adjust wages and prices to ever-changing conditions. But centralized administration cannot cope with this task. It lacks the flexibility and the resistance to the political pressures of the market mechanism, and such attempts to control wages and prices regularly break down in an administrative nightmare. Wage and price guidelines and guideposts have been greatly discredited, but they are proposed again from time to time out of sheer desperation.

Similarly desperate (without hope) is "jawboning"—an attempt to stop an inflation that has been going on for some time and is universally expected to continue. Jawboning is the properly sarcastic technical term for attempting to pursuade the public, even while they are experiencing on-going inflation, that the inflation is ending, so that people will stop raising wages and prices. This is attacking the problem precisely the wrong way around. We must stop the inflation first. Only when the public sees that the inflation has stopped will people stop expecting inflation to continue.

Recently, some superior anti-inflation *incentive* plans have been proposed, based on the recognition of a flaw in our economic system that makes inflation possible in the absence of excess demand. This flaw is what must be corrected, and this is why the solution to inflation does not lie in restraining total spending or in substituting administrative controls for the market regulation of wages and prices.

The flaw is an upward pressure on wages and prices resulting from the perfectly understandable neglect, by each price or wage setter, of the social harm his or her wage or price increase is contributing to the total national inflation. As long as consumers are not made to pay for the social harm, they will not take it into account.

Economists have developed a remedy for this kind of problem. A charge on pollutors that corresponds to the social harm resulting from their pollution can make them take the social harm into account. The Tax Based Income Policies (TIPs) proposed by Henry Wallich and Sidney Weintraub (1971) apply the same principle to the discouragement of inflationary wage increases. This should hold down costs and therefore prices. But all of these plans, as well as the Wage Increase Permit Plan (WIPP) recently proposed by Abba P. Lerner (1978), fail to satisfy condition (2), because they focus the anti-inflation charge or incentive only on *wages*—not on profits. This makes the plans unacceptable to labor and therefore inapplicable in a democratic society.

MAP—the market anti-inflation plan

Most of the wage-oriented TIPs, with varying forms of incentive, call on government to set the level of the anti-inflation charge. But again, this task is too great for government to handle. The market mechanism is required not only to *transmit* a government-set anti-inflation incentive to the competing and bargaining wage and price setters in the economy. The market mechanism is also needed to *set the level of the incentive,* and to *adjust the level* continuously to the ever-changing inflationary pressure it is designed to offset. This last task, if placed on government, would result in a legislative nightmare to rival the administrative nightmare of wage–price guidelines and guideposts.

The Market Anti-inflation Accounting Plan is a device that can be used to mobilize the market mechanism for *all* of these tasks. MAP maps out the route we must take to cure our inflation and its offspring—stagflation.

The basic idea of MAP is to correct the flaw in our economy by translating the *social harm* from the inflationary element in wage and price increases into a *private cost* that is charged directly to the firm, and to do this through the market mechanism, which avoids administrative control or regulation of wages or prices. MAP leaves wage and price levels to be freely determined by the market or by bargaining (as they are now), permitting market influences to affect only the dollar *Net Sales* or direct factor payments by the firm (gross sales minus purchases from other firms). Since Net Sales consists of *combined* profits and wages, this clears MAP of any suspicion of bias and satisfies "fairness" condition (2).

Prices rise (which is what we mean by inflation) when total national dollar Net Sales increases faster than total national (net) real output. This also means that national Net Sales per unit of input increases faster than national net output per unit of input, or productivity. A device that would prevent every firm from increasing its Net Sales per unit of input by more than the national increase in productivity would stop the inflation. But this would fulfill only condition (1). It would *freeze* the economy, preventing the adjustments of *relative* Net Sales (the relative wages and profits), which are essential to the efficient working of a free and unregimented economy.

functional relative changes and nonfunctional inflationary increases

To achieve condition (3), MAP must eliminate the nonfunctional, *inflationary* increases (which tend to raise all wages and prices, serving no social purpose) without interfering with the functional *relative* changes in wages and prices.

As relative prices change, some firms will find their *Net Sales* per unit of input (of productive resources) growing *more* than the national average *net output* per unit of input (productivity). In such cases, it will be essential for other firms to offset this gain by having their Net Sales per unit of input grow correspondingly *less* than national average productivity.

a counter-inflationary incentive

A counter-inflationary incentive must be devised to achieve this relationship. Furthermore, since an inflation affects *all* Net Sales, the counter-inflationary incentive must be applied to all Net Sales. Then it will not interfere with the *relative* changes in Net Sales.

The counter-inflationary incentive must be just strong enough to make total national Net Sales increase at the same rate as total national net output. The rate of inflation will then be zero. This gives MAP the necessary weapon to achieve objective (3).

anti-inflation accounting credit

Only the market can tell us what is the appropriate strength of the counter-inflationary incentive, but MAP can harness the market mechanism for this task. MAP does this by creating *a new commodity*—"MAP Credit"—to be traded on the market. Each firm would be required to *buy* MAP Credit in an amount equal to the *excess* of its Net Sales above the national average net output (in relation to its net inputs), or to *sell* such "Credit" in an amount equal to the *deficit* of its Net Sales below the national average net output (in relation to its net inputs). The market would set the equilibrium price of this "Credit."

The free market price of the "Credit" (just like any other price) would discourage demand and encourage supply until they become equal. This means that it would discourage *excess* Net Sales and encourage *deficits* in Net Sales until they become equal and just cancel each other. Total Net Sales and total net output would then be increasing at the same rate, and there would be no inflation. The free market price of MAP Credit *is* the incentive we need. It would be the exact strength required, and it would be continuously adjusted by the market as conditions change.

All firms would be free to make their individual Net Sales as high or as low as they wish, after taking into account what they pay or receive for the "Credit" they buy or sell. Firms would be induced by the price of the "Credit" to set their Net Sales—and thereby their wages and prices—freely at the levels required for an inflation-free economy.

In an *expectational deflation,* such as the one that occurred in the 1930s, all this could be reversed and the equilibrium price of "Credit" could be negative. Firms with deficit Net Sales would be required to sell their surplus "Credit" at the negative price. (The language could be reversed, too. Firms with "deficit Net Sales" would be required to buy "MAP Debit.")

a self-deflating inflation deflator

Extra "Credit" would permit a firm to enjoy greater Net Sales. The higher the inflationary expectations, the more would firms be willing to pay for additional "Credit" (or would insist on being paid for spare "Credit"), the higher would be the price of "Credit," and the stronger would be the counter-inflationary incentive (the price of "Credit"). MAP thus turns the inflationary pressure against itself jujitsu fashion.

An important result would be that as the inflationary pressure is weakened, the price of "Credit" would fall and the counter-inflationary pressure would also weaken. As MAP deflates the inflation, it is itself deflated. When the inflation and the expectation of inflation stop altogether, the price of "Credit" would fall to zero (or to whatever counter-inflationary pressure may still be required to offset any remaining upward pressures on wages and prices other than inflationary expectations).

As people read this book, their conception of MAP will proceed through distinct phases. It will begin with a phase of pure and simple disbelief. The idea of a solution to inflation is too incredible even to contemplate. Then, it will proceed to the "it may have a point" phase, and they will begin to substitute the MAP framework for the normal economic framework, which has difficulty even admitting the existence of stagflation. Next, the theoretical "it is right, but practically, it's impossible" stage will be reached. At that point, they will be ready to consider the implementation problems.

The next phase will arrive slowly. Finally, they will reach the "it can be done" phase, and the book will have served its purpose. MAP—which at first may have seemed to be a revolutionary dream—will be seen as not so novel after all and will be recognized as a simple variation of a well-established and familiar device—the market!

MAP's central and most astonishing miracle—fixing the *total* increase in Net Sales (and its *average* increase per unit of input) while leaving free each firm's *actual* increase in Net Sales per unit of input—is exactly what the free market accomplishes for many items all the time. The free market, by setting the price of each commodity so that the total supply is equal to the total demand, also makes the *average* quantity demanded of each good per customer equal to the average amount of that good available per customer. At the same time, it leaves free the *actual* amount demanded (and bought) by each customer after he or she has weighed all the costs and benefits. The only difference is that the market, with which we are so familiar that it tends to become invisible, thus far has not included "increases in Net Sales" (in the form of MAP Credit) as one of the myriad of commodities for which it performs this service.

The final question will be: Why hasn't anyone thought of this before? It's so simple. To that question, we have no answer other than to suggest that we seldom look for answers right under our noses; instead, we conjure up dragons of enormous dimensions and then struggle to conquer them. We can only repeat that MAP seems to us to be the logical conclusion of both the arguments in favor of an incomes policy and the arguments in favor of a monetary rule, and there are some signs of the beginnings of a rapprochement—a mutual movement toward the acceptance of a synthesis of these two viewpoints.

Until recently, it was too heretical for a monetarist to suggest that the solution to inflation would require anything more than holding down the money supply, or for an incomes policy enthusiast to admit that the market was a reasonable method of control. However, advocates of both views seem to be moderating their positions. Milton Friedman (1974) recently stated that controlling the money supply may not be politically possible and that another method must be found. Meanwhile, direct regulation has acquired an increasingly tarnished reputation. Calls for deregulation are heard more frequently, and the advantages of the market mechanism are becoming better understood. We hope the extremes will meet in an acceptance of some variant of MAP.

2

inflation: what it is and what causes it

Inflation can mean blowing air into a balloon. When the balloon is blown up, it expands. Filled with a gas lighter than air, it rises, and the children think it great fun. If the gas leaks out, the balloon deflates. It contracts, falls to the ground, and loses its beautiful shape—making the children sad.

inflation: what it is

Applied to the world of business and economics, inflation has come to mean the condition that occurs when the pressure on prices puts a dangerous strain on the fabric of the economy, like a balloon that is blown up too far. Or it can mean the condition of prices rising higher and higher, like a lighter-than-air balloon. The economy is then often declared to be "overheated" and is fated to fall to earth like a fire balloon when the fuel is gone. Or inflation can be compared to a hydrogen or a helium balloon that rises very high and expands farther in the lower pressure of the upper atmosphere until finally it bursts and crashes. The fire-balloon analogy most closely fits the economic movements of business cycles in which "booms" when prices rise are followed by "busts" when prices fall. The hydrogen-helium balloon represents runaway or "galloping" inflations—the "hyperinflations" in which prices rise to hundreds, thousands, millions, or even billions of times what they have been, and an economic collapse follows.

When this happened in Germany in 1923, prices rose to more than 10 billion times what they had been a year before. In the Confederacy during the Civil War, prices rose "only" by some 20,000 percent. Life became uncomfortable. Production was disorganized. Many people were ruined; others made enormous profits. Ultimately, nearly everybody suffered severely in the resulting chaos, as more and more people, instead of staying at their jobs, rushed to buy something—anything—before prices rose still further. Less and less goods were produced. There was a general impoverishment in real goods, while everyone became a "millionaire" in depreciated money.

descriptions of inflation

Technical descriptions of inflation can be much more complicated, but they convey the same idea. Such descriptions attempt to answer explicitly how

7

much the price level, or "the average price," rises if some prices increase more than others, or to determine whether the price level rises at all if some prices increase while others decrease.

There are many answers to these questions. For different purposes, the prices of different combinations of goods are relevant. Consumers are really less concerned about prices in general than they are about the prices of the goods they buy. Only a custom-made index could measure the prices of goods preferred by individual consumers. Such indexes are administratively impossible, but to allow for different interests, we have a wholesale price index, a retail price index, a consumer price index, an urban consumer price index, a rural consumer price index, a value added price index, a GNP deflator, a Net National Product (NNP) deflator, and many more.

Each of these in turn can be produced in different ways with varying degrees of carefulness and completeness. Even if there is agreement both on what is to be included and on the accuracy of the individual price quotations on which the calculations are to be based, the index still can be constructed in different ways. It might be designed to show the change in the cost of the quantities bought at the earlier or at the later of the dates being compared, or it might be based on some further averaging of these two computations.

To the reader's probable relief, we will not discuss these technical details—other than to say that the index of inflation which MAP is designed to stabilize is the NNP deflator. This applies only to currently produced goods and services, takes in all of them, and avoids all double counting.

Stabilizing the NNP deflator will not stabilize the other indexes precisely. Nor is it desirable to prevent temporary fluctuations in the NNP deflator itself, which only indicate temporary fluctuations in total output.

Fortunately, all the different prices in the economy are kept sufficiently in line by the possibility of producers and consumers switching from one good to another, so that all the indexes do not differ too much from each other. The NNP deflator cannot reflect the different experiences of every consumer of every item. Nevertheless, everybody knows whether an inflation is going on or not.

the effects of inflation

The current condition in the United States is one of inflation. (We suspect there is little disagreement about this observation.) It is in no way the hyperinflation that devastated Germany in the 1920s, but neither is it a "creeping" inflation. It is somewhere in between—perhaps a trot or a canter, but not quite a gallop. It is increasing at the rate of about 10 percent each year.

By itself, such a rate of price increase does not disrupt or disorganize the economy. It does not interfere drastically with the efficient production and distribution of all the goods and services that we enjoy. Indeed, while the population has been growing steadily, the quantity of goods and services we are currently producing and consuming has also been increasing almost every year, not only in terms of total output but also in terms of the amount of goods and services available per person, although it has not increased as much as might have been expected.

This does not mean that such an inflation is having no effect on the economy. If prices rise at a rate of 10 percent a year, compounded interest would make them double in about 7 years. In 14 years, prices would double twice—they would be 4 times what they are now. Anybody with a fixed income would be able to buy only one-half as much in 7 years, and only one-quarter as much in 14 years. Pensioners with fixed pensions would become impoverished. In real terms, they would have lost one-half or three-quarters of their pensions.

Because of its distributional effects, even a moderate inflation is bad. The evil is usually greatly exaggerated, but that does not stop it from being a bad thing. Since the essence of inflation is rising prices, it is bad for the buyers who have to pay the higher prices and who are made poorer to that degree. But since somebody always receives the higher price, the buyer's loss is balanced by the seller's gain. Nevertheless, we often hear accounts of the evils of inflation as if there were only buyers and no sellers of goods and services in the country.

In his State of the Union message in 1970, President Nixon said that in the course of 10 years the government of the United States had incurred deficits amounting to $57 billion, which had resulted in an inflation that had raised the cost of living of the average American family of four by $200 a month. This would amount to about $600 billion,[1] so that it appears to have brought about a loss to American families of more than 10 times the taxes that would have covered the deficit, and to continue to burden them to the extent of $120 billion a year (or more than twice the cumulative deficit over the 10 sinful years)—a very bad business indeed. In this argument, Nixon failed to count the corresponding identical gain to the sellers of the goods bought by American families. The incomes of these sellers had increased by the same $600 billion and would continue to earn an additional $120 billion per annum in the future.

The President could simply have reversed this argument and patted himself and his predecessors on the back for having obtained such a great increase in the incomes of the American public at the mere cost of $57 billion in deficits. This reversed argument is, of course, no better than the original. The two arguments completely cancel each other out. Any proper accounting must consider both the higher payments and the higher receipts, which are two sides of the same transactions.

Inflation, however, is not quite as unpopular as we might judge from public statements, which not only exaggerate its evils but liberally attribute to inflation many sins of which it is completely innocent. Although everybody grumbles about higher prices when they are buying goods or services, they are pleased, or at least relieved, when they increase their profits by raising the prices of what they sell, or obtain higher wages for their work or higher interest or dividend payments from their investments.

---

[1]50 million (families) × $100 (a month—the average increase over the 10 years) × 12 (months in a year) × 10 (years) = $600 billion.

The true unpopularity of inflation results from concentrating on the *particular* prices individuals must pay for what they buy rather than on prices in general or on *all* prices. I suffer from inflation only if the prices of what I buy rise more than the prices of what I sell. Stated more generally, this means I suffer only from *relative* price increases and then only if the prices of what I buy rise *relatively* to the prices of what I sell. The latter includes my income, which is the price I receive for the sale of my work and the services of the property I own. (Of course, I *gain* if I am on the other side of the fence.)

"pure" inflation

In a "pure" inflation, in which *all* prices rise in the same proportion, there would be no *relative* price increases (and, of course, no relative price decreases). Therefore, a pure inflation could hurt no one (and also could not benefit anyone).

Is such a pure and harmless inflation possible, or even conceivable? In the first place, even if prices rise uniformly, the price of a next-year item rises *relatively* to the price of a this-year item, so that producers of goods for future sale will gain from the higher price, while future buyers will lose. However, economists have shown that the market could neutralize these relative price changes, and eliminate the gains and losses, by increasing the interest rate to allow for the inflation rate. This would offset the gain to the seller, because a greater amount of interest would be lost while waiting for the future sale; it would offset the loss to the buyer, because a greater amount of interest would be earned over the same waiting period. Thus, the change in the interest would negate the apparent relative price change.

One price that cannot be "inflation proofed" by the interest rate is the price of a dollar—which is always $1. The rate of interest that can protect or restore the "purity" of the inflation for all other prices can only *measure* the rate of decrease over time in the purchasing power of the dollar—its usefulness in buying goods. The interest rate indicates how much we have to discount future dollars in comparing their purchasing power to that of today's dollar. In a severe inflation, this decrease can be very serious. It becomes more expensive to hold the shrinking dollars, and the public contrives to hold *less purchasing power* in dollars, although more $1 bills (or even $1,000 bills) may be required. Less *real money* (less current purchasing power) is held, and this can result in a serious loss of the benefits in the convenience derived from holding money. (We do, in fact, normally hold billions of dollars for the sake of this convenience.) In the German hyperinflation in 1923, the expensiveness of this convenience led workers to reduce it so much that they had to take time off from work to rush to buy goods and services rather than hold on to the depreciating currency for hours.

However, economists have also figured out how to avoid this damage from inflation. If the monetary authority were to pay *interest* at the market rate on cash money held by the public, holding money would not be made any more costly by the inflation and none of the benefits that the use of money contributes to the efficiency of the economy would be lost. The apparent gift (the interest payments) to the money holders would do nothing more than compensate them for the benefits they would have lost by holding the money while prices rose. The burden on the government for making this "gift" would amount to no more than what would otherwise have been obtained from the money holders, who would have been paid depreciating money for whatever the government bought with the money when it was issued. The inflation could still be kept "pure."

But the maintenance of such a "pure" and "harmless" inflation, which changes no *relative* prices, would in fact be a terrible plague. It would prevent our market mechanism from performing its function of inducing consumers to shift from consumption that involves increased sacrifice by others to consumption that involves reduced sacrifice (because it could not make the former relatively more expensive). Maintaining such a "pure" inflation would also prevent the market mechanism from inducing producers to shift from goods and services that provide reduced benefits to other goods and services that provide increased benefits (because it could not make the latter relatively more profitable). This is because it is precisely the *relative* increases and decreases—the *relative* changes in prices and wages—that constitute the incentives and guides to consumers and producers that have paved the way for economic progress. Freeing the markets has made possible the adjustments that have resulted in the enormous growth of output and living standards in the last few hundred years.

The best of all possible worlds, if we must have some inflation, would be a "pure" inflation in a different sense. It would be an inflation that did not raise all prices evenly but permitted the *relative* wage and price changes needed to bring about the appropriate adjustments in all wages and prices to reflect the changes in tastes, in incomes, in technologies, and in the availabilities of all productive resources.

For such an economy to work, it would only be necessary for everybody to know the rate of inflation. They could then conduct business in the usual way and merely adjust every price to reflect the amount of inflation from some base date to the date of payment. (Lots of little hand calculators are now available that can make this calculation at the touch of a button.) But such an adjustment is possible only if the *adjusted* price is meaningful enough to be an accurate guideline indicating how much of the item in question should be demanded or supplied. Hidden behind this glib solution are the assumptions that *everybody* has made the appropriate adjustment to the same degree of inflation, that everybody has had sufficient time to make preparations to buy and sell these items at the correctly anticipated prices, that all the prices set by others (which here would mean by everyone else) have been determined appropriately, and that all this is also true of the production of the instruments of production, and the production of the instruments of production of the instruments of production of all complementary and competing items in the economy. This however does not stump ingenious economists, who point out that everything would work out well given the assumption of rational expectations.

Only slightly less fanciful than such rational expectations would be an economy in which money prices were not considered at all, except in settling accounts. All decisions related to buying and selling, producing and consuming, would be made only on the basis of the *ratios* between the prices of goods, considering the goods two at a time. These ratios are sometimes called "relative prices." If we could conceive of the "relative price" of every possible pair of alternative products being considered, the proper decisions could conceivably be made quite efficiently. This is actually the way business transactions were made in barter societies before money was developed. These societies could not have become very advanced economically without developing the practical economies that result from using money prices to make rational economic choices. But that fact does not restrain mathematical economists from calculating the equations and the equilibria of the most complex imaginary barter economies.

The practical economies that develop from the use of money result when the dollar (or some other money unit) becomes a simple representation of *all* the alternatives to a particular purchase. This can be built up in the mind of the buyer only by experience over a considerable period of time, during which prices are permitted to establish expected "natural" values or limited ranges of "normal" values.

Mini-calculators could be used to adjust to a "pure" inflation only as long as there were no significant relative changes in prices—that is, as long as there were no significant adjustments to the inevitable changes in tastes, techniques, and availabilities. If prices and wages did become appropriately adjusted, the corrected prices would become less and less meaningful as the prices of the alternative purchases changed in different ways and were less and less usefully represented by the figure tendered by the mini-calculators.

What follows from all this is that only a money of stable buying power can provide the practical economies in terms of economic calculations to make a complex economy workable. Devices for adjusting to the inflation can work only if substitutes for stable prices are provided. These substitutes are inferior, and if they are used persistently they become "inferiorer and inferiorer." They do not successfully enable us to live with inflation. We must *cure* the inflation. To cure the inflation, we have to remove the cause. But first we must find the cause.

the cause of inflation

A cause is that link in a chain of causes and further causes at which point we stop asking about still further causes. Sometimes we stop because it is considered improper to continue, sometimes we stop because we are exhausted—and sometimes we stop because we do not know what more to ask.

When we try to solve a problem, we continue along the chain and stop when we reach a link about which we can do something that will help to solve the problem that started the chain of questions in the first place. No search for further causes is then necessary, because we have reached a point where we believe the *control* can be instituted. At this point, we say we have discovered *the cause* of the trouble, and we start to devise a solution.

In looking for the cause of inflation, we will reach the stopping point very quickly if we find that prices in general are rising because the economy is operating at full capacity and total spending in the economy is increasing at a rate that is clearly greater than is required to buy all the potential output of the economy at current prices. We can then say that an excessive increase in total spending is the cause of this inflation and that if the government would stop this excessive increase in spending, the inflation would be alleviated or even cured.

For the monetarists, who also believe (for related but more complicated reasons) that restraint in the money supply could cure the inflation, it is only natural to suggest that the cause of inflation is related to the money supply. Others, who believe that only wage and price controls could stop the inflation, disagree. In the ensuing debate, some economists have yielded to the temptation to attribute causality to what happens earlier, confusing causality with priority. But expectations permit anticipated future changes to influence present (near-future) decisions, laying traps for those who yield to such temptations.

Our present inflation does not bring us to "the cause" by such a short chain. Instead, we find a full circle in which we can go around from cause to cause forever and ever. Prices rise *because* wages rise *because* spending rises *because* prices rise *because*. . . .

To pick one of these links out of the circle and declare it to be *the cause* is arbitrary and unconvincing, until it can be shown that treating that particular cause would actually lead to a successful solution of our inflation problem.

In the vicious circle in which prices, wages, and (total) spending chase each other, it seems that if any *one* of the members of the cast were stopped, the choreography would be upset and the race would come to an end. In Chapter 3, we will examine past inflation remedies that seem to have been based on the principle of concentrating on only one of the three runners in the futile inflationary race. There, we will try to show why all of these attempts came to grief. MAP indicates how an *integrated* approach—and only an integrated approach—that takes all three elements into account at the same time can offer a solution.

Since we have defined a cause as the link (in a chain of causes) that we think we can control—and therefore as the point at which we can begin to solve the problem—our suggestion that inflation has a cure implies that we have found "the cause." That cause is a *socially faulty private accounting system.* A necessary condition for increasing efficiency as well as satisfying legitimate expectations "fairly" is the achievement of a stable price level. Individuals cannot be expected to take this societal goal into account when they make decisions. The result is that billions of pricing decisions are not necessarily designed to produce a stable price level. The reasons for this and the precise nature of the process need not concern us at this point. The process may result from expectations due to past government actions or from quite different reasons. These considerations are irrelevant for our solution, and therefore are not associated with the cause. The *flaw,* which is our *cause* of inflation, is eliminated by our *cure,* which is the Market Anti-inflation *incentive*—the price of MAP Credit.

3

the history of
anti-inflation
policies:
*money and the limits
to money management*

Historically, anti-inflation policy has been a variation on two themes: (1) regulation of the money supply, and (2) controls over wages and prices. Again and again, nations have turned to one or both of these "remedies" in various combinations in an attempt to cure inflation.

the money supply

Controls have never been a favorite of economists, who (we suspect), have all drunk deeply of the classical doctrine that inflation—a decline in the value of money—is everywhere and always a monetary phenomenon (just as the price of potatoes is everywhere and always a potato phenomenon). Thus, within every economist lurk some vestiges of the monetarist belief that if the money supply is properly managed, controls are unnecessary and can only make things worse.

Some relationship between the quantity of money and the price level was probably recognized as soon as "money" was a well-defined concept and its supply was controllable. Neither condition is easily met, and may not yet have been fully satisfied.

Neither paper currency nor banks existed until long after money was in widespread use. In fact, early "money" was not very similar to the money we know today. Money first developed as merely the most useful *unit of account* in which to express relative values. Generally, money consisted of the most important commodity in the economy. Horses, pigs, and chickens all served as early monies. No regulation of the use of such commodities as money was possible.

credit money

As a means of facilitating trade, live commodity monies had their drawbacks. It was rather difficult to pay half a horse and preserve the essence of horseness. Thus, "inert" commodity monies, which could be divided easily, replaced "live" commodity monies. Gold was the most common inert commodity money in circulation. The very use of gold demonstrates that the connection between the supply of money and inflation was recognized, at least implicitly, at an early date. Gold was used rather than sand because gold

14

was severely limited in quantity. Large increases in the quantity of gold were impossible and therefore could not cause large increases in the gold prices of commodities. The supply of gold could not be managed or controlled by any authority. It depended on the vagaries of new discovery and plunder. (Many monetarists would argue that these vagaries are preferable to the vagaries of government control.) Increases in gold money were not subject to governmental manipulation.

The next step in the technological advance of money was the use of "gold receipts" rather than gold itself. Money was now no longer composed solely of a tangible commodity, like gold. Money also consisted of *credit,* and the supply of credit could be regulated. Initially, no regulation was instituted.

The introduction of credit money probably went something like this. Storing gold was a dangerous business: People worried about its security and possible loss. It was natural for individuals to look for a safe place to store their gold. Generally, they left it with the local goldsmith, who had a well-protected vault for the gold he used in his work. Each person who stored gold in the goldsmith's vault obtained a receipt—a certificate indicating the gold had been received—which had to be returned to get the gold back. People soon discovered that it was easier to make a payment for something by presenting the certificate instead of returning the certificate to the goldsmith, removing the gold from the goldsmith's vault, and carrying it with them to make the payment. The person who received this gold would then merely return it to the goldsmith and obtain an identical certificate. This was the first use of certificate money, which represented—or stood for, or was as good (for this purpose) as—the gold. A certificate was accepted as payment because it was believed to be *100 percent backed by gold* in the goldsmith's vault.

Goldsmiths soon realized that only a small percentage of their gold was needed at any one time to meet normal withdrawals. Therefore, they could profitably and safely loan out some of the gold. They found they could make such loans in the form of certificates, which were *issued in addition to* the certificates they had already issued in exchange for the gold they actually held in their vaults. The borrowers and those who accepted these certificates as payment could not distinguish between certificates issued as loans and certificates issued in exchange for solid gold. All certificates were still considered to be 100 percent backed by gold.

This procedure worked well and benefited everyone. The borrowers received needed credit, the goldsmith made a profit, and those who held certificates had faith in their "100 percent gold backing"—*as long as everyone believed in the soundness of the system and did not come to redeem their certificates at the same time.* However, this was an important condition. If everyone did try to redeem their certificates at the same time, the system would break down.

This development completed the transformation of money into its modern form. Some of the money was actually credit. Its supply could be increased by issuing certificates as loans and could be decreased by canceling certificates when loans were repaid. If too many certificates were issued as loans, this could enable buyers to attempt to purchase more goods and services than the economy could produce. Such *excess demand* would cause prices to rise and the result would be inflation—*demand inflation*. (It would be just as if too much gold had been discovered.) Conversely, a net repayment of the loans would decrease the number of certificates in circulation, which could result in a *deficient demand* for goods and services and cause depression or deflation.

The early history of these monies was filled with booms and busts. When times were good and everyone had faith in the money, loans increased and the supply of certificate money expanded. Periodically, however, people became worried about the soundness of the certificates and redeemed them for solid gold. As their vaults began to empty, the goldsmiths issued fewer new loans. The economy soon floundered. The money supply contracted, the demand for goods and services was reduced, and depression resulted.

money management

There are two possible ways to interpret the next step in the history of money. One interpretation is that the government saw that it could get something for nothing and claimed the sole right to issue credit money. A second interpretation is that the transfer to the government of the sole right to issue money was the result of a need to standardize the various kinds and denominations of "certificates" and to avoid these inflations and depressions. At this point, the government, by regulating the supply of credit, could influence the money supply, thereby acquiring the ability—by money management—to create as well as avoid inflations and depressions.

From this arose the famous *quantity theory of money*, which begins with the equation of exchange $MV = PQ$. This tells us that M (the quantity of money) multiplied by V (the velocity of the circulation of money, or the average number of times each dollar is spent) is equal to P (the average price) multiplied by Q (the quantity of goods bought). This is always and everywhere true, because MV is the total amount spent in buying the goods and PQ is the total amount received from selling the same goods. These two amounts cannot be different. They are the same thing—the sum of the money that is changing hands—whether counted as purchases or as sales.

The quantity theory is something quite different from the equation of exchange, although both theories are often represented by the same formula. The quantity theory states that changes in M, the quantity of money, result in proportional changes in P, the average price. This is true only if V and Q do not change (or if they change in exactly the same direction and in the same proportion). But this becomes a reasonable proposition *if we can assume* that over the period in question things in general remain the same—in the sense that neither V, the velocity of circulation, nor Q, the quantity of goods produced and sold, changes significantly. It will then be true that a change in M will bring about a proportional change in P, and we can say that controlling the quantity of money controls the average price or price level. Early classical economists who noted this connection include John Stuart Mill, who wrote in his *Principles of Political Economy* (1848) "The substitution of paper money for metallic currency is a national gain, and further increases of paper beyond this amount is a form of robbery." Similarly, Stanley Jevons (1875) wrote "An expansion of currency occurs one or two years prior to a rise of prices."

when money management works

There is one case in which money control (or spending control) is sufficient. In the case of a *pure demand inflation,* which is accurately described as "too much money chasing too few goods," the cause of the inflation is an excess of total spending in the economy. This occurs when all the spenders— individuals, businesses, the government, and all other private organizations—are, in total, spending too much. In effect, the spenders are trying to buy more goods and services than the economy can make available. This inevitably bids up prices. At higher prices, a greater volume of spending is required to buy what the economy *can* provide. If the increase in prices catches up with the excess spending, prices will stop rising. But whatever caused total spending to become excessive in the first place may continue to operate, so that *even at higher and rising prices,* buyers will continue to try to buy more than the economy can supply. As long as this goes on, the demand inflation will continue. The obvious cure is to stop the continuing excess demand, which means removing its cause. This is the responsibility of the government. If it wishes to stop the inflation, it must bring an end to the continuing excessive spending—either by stopping the excessive increase in its own spending or by inducing others to stop the excessive increase in *their* spending.

Two basic measures to check the increase in nongovernment spending are to increase taxes, so that taxpayers have less left to spend, or to make it harder for spenders to borrow money. The instruments are fiscal and monetary restraint. Unfortunately, few inflations remain pure demand inflations, even if they begin that way. An inflation quickly becomes *expectational* and acquires a life of its own. Thus, even if whatever caused the total spending to be excessive is terminated, the inflation will continue on its own momentum.

Even more unfortunate is the fact that expectational inflation can also exist with less than full employment. In such a case, prices, wages, money incomes, and the quantity of money all increase, just as they do in a pure demand inflation, even though it is no longer true that "too much money is chasing too few goods." Spenders are not trying to buy more than the economy can produce. There is significant unemployment of both workers and productive equipment.

There may be too much spending in some sectors and too little in others, and it is uncertain precisely where full employment begins. However, when we believe that additional production is possible and desirable, but inflation exists, we call the situation *stagflation.*

the practical dilemma

Money control was not always unable to control inflation. This is a new development. In the post-war period, the government, following a Keynesian

economic policy of functional finance, maintained a high level of employment and prosperity for an unprecedented period of time. But then we were
confronted by a new problem. The price level was rising in the absence of
excess demand. The government faced a dilemma; it could take two possible
courses of action. One alternative was to increase the money supply and the
volume of total spending to make it possible for the high employment to
continue. This would "ratify" the higher price level and keep unemployment
low, but it would mean accepting the inflation. The second alternative was to
hold down the money supply as an anti-inflation measure. This would not
merely "ratify" but even *increase* the unemployment.

The federal government tried a bit of both policies. They increased the
money supply and total spending, but not enough to keep up with the rising
prices. Money became tight because the demand for money increased due
to the higher prices. This had little effect on the inflation. The money supply
and spending failed to keep up with the continuing increase in prices, thereby
creating a credit crunch, a depression, and increasingly severe unemployment. The monetary authorities then reluctantly yielded to pressure and
turned to the first alternative to rescue the economy. To head off the impending calamities, they increased the money supply and total spending, even
though this "ratified" the inflationary price and wage increases. Some economists suggest that this means that holding down the money supply was
never really tried; others hold that this policy cannot be used. We side with
the latter.

directions of causation

We have already seen that holding down total spending does not work if the
price increases are due not to excess spending but to built-in expectations. In
this case, there is *not enough spending* to maintain a satisfactory level of
employment and output.

Instead of an increase in money and spending causing prices to rise,
the opposite seems true. *Rising prices seem to be causing the increase in
money and spending!*

A closer look shows, however, that the new phenomenon is not really
the reversal of a linear direction of causation. That would leave us with a cost
push theory of inflation, which does not explain what makes the costs keep
on pushing. This is no improvement over the linear demand pull theory,
which does not explain what makes the excess demand keep on pulling.

The new phenomenon is an inflation in which the causation is not linear
at all but *circular,* so that each item can be called a cause of any other item in
the circle—indirectly, if not directly. Wages rise because workers have to
keep up with rising prices to maintain the standard of living. Prices rise
because businesses have to keep up with rising costs (from the increasing
wages) to maintain solvency. The money and the spending rise because the
government must increase them to keep up with prices to maintain a
tolerable level of employment in the economy. To advise government to do
otherwise is simply a "classical" waste of breath, just as it would be futile to
advise labor not to raise wages or business not to raise prices. Labor,

business, and government would each claim with equal sincerity that it could react in no other way because the other parties "started it." No search for leads and lags can help in the slightest, nor can any priority be given to any one of the three runners in this inflationary race. Each must run as fast as the others to keep from falling behind.

What *started* this vicious circle is an interesting historical and philosophical topic, but like the chicken-and-egg conundrum, it does not help us break the vicious circle. Whether the self-fulfilling expectations originally resulted from the conclusions that decision makers drew about the effects of increases in the money supply or from changing institutional structures in the post-war era is an infinitely debatable question that need not concern us here. Both views recognize that no matter how they started, increases in the money supply and total spending and in prices and wages have now all become interrelated parts of a system of indeterminate leads and lags.

The practical fact is that we have not managed to handle this problem. Our indecision between the two alternative, unsatisfactory policies has led to a "stop and go" oscillation between the classical policy of monetary restraint and the Keynesian policy of monetary adjustment—between succumbing to threats of intolerable unemployment and succumbing to threats of escalating inflation. This vacillation has led to stagflation—the combination of inflation and economic stagnation—and to a dizzying urge to jump once more into the morass of controls. The story it tells is of a flaw in our economy, which the instruments developed thus far have been unable to correct.

a flaw in the
economic mechanism

The Keynesian innovations (1936) were able to restore and maintain a reasonably satisfactory level of employment in a depression where the classical, *automatic,* full-employment equilibrium had been stymied. Keynes provided a remedy for the failure of prices (which includes wages) to fall far enough and fast enough, in response to a deficiency in demand, to raise the *buying power* of the existing quantity of money and the associated level of total spending to a satisfactory level.

The Keynesian remedy was simple: *Increase the total level of spending in the economy to compensate for the lack of a decrease in prices.* Like Mohammed and the Mountain, if the prices could not be adjusted to the spending, the spending would have to be adjusted to the prices.

Now the flaw in our economy has suffered a mutation. Prices no longer merely fail to fall. They continue to *rise,* caught in the self-fulfilling expectational inflation (however this was initiated). Instead of trying to maintain their real rewards by refusing to allow wages or prices to *fall,* labor and business are now trying to maintain their real rewards by refusing to *fall behind* in the inflation. Governments seem to have an incurable propensity to treat inflation as if it were always due to too much total spending, and so they do not provide enough total spending to keep up with the rising wages and prices. This creates the stagflation.

when money management fails

Trying to cure expectational inflation by restraints on total spending works only by creating or increasing unemployment.

Three problems result from this approach. One is the continued technological change in the credit industry, which complicates the government's task of managing the money supply. Whenever the monetary authorities attempt to put the brakes on the money *supply,* an initial squeeze is felt. But new credit instruments—money substitutes—soon develop which circumvent the restraints by decreasing the *demand* for "plain" money (M_1). Eurodollars, CD's, and NOW accounts are examples. This has led to broader and broader definitions of the money supply ($M_2, M_3, \ldots,$ etc.) to include the credit instruments that provide substitutes for plain money. This relatively minor complication can be dealt with by making a compensatingly larger adjustment in M_1, by action on the money substitutes, and by complementary fiscal policy.

The second problem is one of equity. A restrictive spending policy does not affect all parties equally. The burden of the induced depression falls mainly on those businesses that depend more on credit or that produce the less urgently demanded goods and services that people give up in a depression. The heaviest burden falls on the workers who lose their jobs. There is no good reason why these groups should have to bear most of the burden. If a burden is unavoidable (which we basically question), we should be able to design a program that distributes this burden more equally.

The third problem with a restrictive spending policy is one of social efficiency. The unemployment and the decrease in production that result from restrictive monetary policies are only instruments to reduce wage and price increases. The success of restrictive monetary policy depends on increasing unemployment to reduce the rate of wage increases, which reduces cost increases, which reduces the price increases and lowers the expectations that drive expectational inflation. This mechanism is intolerably inefficient. It is so costly and so disruptive that the policy is always discarded in despair before it can achieve its objective. This despair is one of the reasons governments repeatedly resort to wage and price controls.

These arguments are not new, but they acquire special relevance because MAP, working in conjunction with monetary spending policy, can reduce and eventually eliminate wage and price increases *without depending on increased unemployment* to achieve this task. MAP will make monetary policy more efficient, so that it will not have to be abandoned before the task of curing the inflation is completed.

4

the history of anti-inflation policies:
controls and incomes policies

Economists and politicians have long recognized the dilemma posed by monetary management, yet because of a fear of controls, they continue to cling to the hope that monetary spending control—however bad—will work. Their hopes have failed regularly, and controls have repeatedly been resorted to in the fight against inflation. As early as 4,000 years ago in Babylon, the Code of Hammurabi imposed rigid controls over both wages and prices. Such controls were also used in China, Greece, and the Roman Empire. The sanctions associated with these controls were often rather strong; individuals who exceeded the "guidelines" set forth in the Roman controls were executed.

Wage and price controls were employed in the post BC era at intermittent intervals, generally after enough time had elapsed for people to forget their last experience with controls.

the natural history of controls

Over time, wage and price controls were continually turned to for two quite different reasons. The first might be called a lack of knowledge of how much total spending is enough. Money and credit is needed to facilitate trade. When increases in output are possible, an increase in money and credit benefits everyone. Trade is facilitated, production increases, and the issuing authority generates revenue at no cost. But it is difficult to know when a further increase in money stops being helpful and becomes inflationary. Generally, issuing authorities expand the money supply beyond the point at which inflation begins. At that point, they could either stop issuing money, in which case they would lose the revenue they were gaining from issuing the money, or they could try to have their cake and eat it too by continuing to increase the money supply and establishing a law that prices could not rise. If quantity could rise, price controls would direct higher demand into higher production; if not, it would create black markets and shortages.

In discussing these controls, it is important to distinguish two types of price controls—specific price controls and general price controls.

21

Specific price controls are usually instituted when there is a "scarcity" of some item. Although they do limit the income redistribution that would occur from a large increase in prices by not allowing prices to rise, specific controls also aggravate the shortage.

An increase in demand or a decrease in supply would result in a rise in price, which would restore the equality between demand and supply. But price control prohibits the price increase. At the lower, controlled price, there are not enough goods and services available for all the consumers to be able to buy as much as they would like, which results in a scarcity. Sometimes the price has already risen, and the price control is enforced to prevent the price from rising still further. In some cases, the control reduces the price to a previous level.

black markets

The first effect of price controls is usually the emergence of a black market, where consumers who are not able to purchase an item at the legal price can pay a higher, illegal price to obtain it. It is hard to prevent this from happening, since both the buyer and the seller benefit from the transaction and nobody else needs to know about it. The item may disappear altogether from the open or "white" market. If substantial black market tendencies decrease "white" market quantities and the black market becomes important and widely used, it becomes a "gray" market and ultimately even a "free" market, in contrast to the official ("unfree") market. The black market, with its attendant evils, is nevertheless an *alleviation* of the damages from price controls. Indeed, as we shall see, the successful repression of the black market would make things worse, not better.

The evil from price controls is not that the official *price* is "unfree" but that the *quantity* we can buy at this price is "unfree." Unless the price control drives the supply entirely to the black market, legitimate sellers have to deal with a demand for more of the item than they have available. They may, of course, only pretend not to exceed the legal price, but in fact raise the price by various subterfuges. They may reduce portions, knowing their customers will not dare to complain. They may insist on tie-in sales, in which a part of the increased price is disguised as payment for high-priced, tied-in goods (which are not controlled). But such subterfuges are very poor solutions to the basic problem. A free price settles at the level at which all who are willing to pay the price can buy the good. At the controlled price, there is not enough of the item to go around. (This does not mean that there never will be shortages in "white markets." In the name of fairness, there are often temporary shortages due to priority restrictions rather than price increases.)

Perfectly honest and scrupulously legalistic sellers are still faced with the problem of who should get more, who should get less, and who should do without. Sellers will be tempted to sell to friends and not to strangers or people they dislike. They may even be tempted to consider their friends those who are better customers and who buy more of the items on which they earn a greater profit. A seller may not even realize that this is very close to the subterfuge of tie-in sales. But even if the seller's intent is good, this practice can be disastrous to the poor (who cannot be such good customers), to strangers, and to any other people to whom a seller decides not to sell.

Often, despite the intended "fairness" of the quantity restriction, the result is quite unfair. A scarce item will be more available to the rich, the charming, and the regular customers, while the poor, the unattractive, and the strangers may find nothing left when they come to buy. Favored customers may be served "under-the counter," as this has come to be called in countries plagued by such price controls. The price control, which was intended to protect the poor from a high price that would restrict them to buying only very little of a scarce item, in effect prevents many of them from purchasing any of the items at all on the legal market. On the black market—where they can buy as much as they can pay for—the price is much higher than the uncontrolled price would have been. This is because (1) only a portion of the scarce item reaches the black market, since many consumers who are able to buy a good cheaply on the legal market at the controlled price purchase more of it than they would have bought in the absence of the price control, and (2) because the black marketeer must be compensated for the additional hazards and costs of operating illegally.

rationing

Even if sellers are honest and law abiding and recognize a social responsibility for the power that has been thrust on them, there is still very little they can do. They will try to allocate scarce goods fairly among different customers, limiting the amount of an item that is sold to any one of them to retain some for all customers. But sellers are not in a position to enforce this at all effectively. A seller cannot tell if a customer asks for his or her allotment more than once, buys from many sellers, or resells an item later for a higher price on the black market. Dissatisfaction with this kind of amateur rationing results in the development of official rationing systems under government auspices. This can be much fairer, since it more or less ensures that everyone has only one ration book, entitling him or her to buy specified amounts of the various rationed items. It is clearly a great improvement over haphazard rationing by shopkeepers of different degrees of competence, as well as different degrees of goodwill.

But discontent still continues to grow. The rationing authority, no matter how great a bureaucracy it builds up, cannot account for the special needs of different individuals or families. It must treat all people as if they were identical. So vegetarians receive meat rations when they would rather have more fruits and vegetables, and carnivorous customers receive the same meat ration, which to them looks much too small, and have little use for their rations of natural or organic foods that the vegetarians covet. Similar wasteful inefficiencies multiply as the money consumers save because they are able to buy the rationed goods at lower, controlled, prices becomes available for them to use to buy other goods. This increase in the demand for uncontrolled goods tends to cause *their* prices to be raised and then to be controlled. At the controlled prices, the demand for these goods, too, eventually exceeds the supply, and these commodities are added to the list of rationed goods.

rationing rationalized

The next stage in the natural history of price controls is the invention of devices to make rationing more flexible. Commodities are rationed in groups, and *ration points* are provided that can be used to obtain different items in a group. The same points can be used for steak and for hamburger (of course, for a greater quantity of hamburger than steak) as well as for fats and butter and milk and cheese. Similarly, instead of different ration points for shirts and socks, there are ration points for clothes. A certain number of points are assigned to a pair of socks, another number of points to a shirt, and so on, so that the available clothes can be distributed more in accordance with the needs and tastes of different consumers.

But when this is done, some of the items remain unsold. Consumers use their points to buy the more popular alternatives among which they are allowed to choose. These more popular items will be in such short supply that customers will not be able to obtain them even though they offer the required number of points according to the rationing plan. We will be back again where we were before rationing was instituted, when we were not able to buy the goods even though we offered the required amount of money according to the controlled price. At this stage in the development of a more and more sophisticated rationing system, if is necessary to keep readjusting the number of points that are required to obtain each controlled item.

A rationing system can progress through still higher stages of rationalization, until it becomes a *second price system*. But long before this stage has been reached, price control is usually abandoned—to the accompaniment of universal cheers.

repressed inflation

The price control we have considered here covers only some of the prices, and most of the effects that we presented in its "natural history" were affected by this fact. If some prices are controlled, those who can obtain the items cheaply will use them wastefully. This results in a still greater shortage of these goods, forcing consumers who are not able to obtain them to shift to less satisfactory—or more expensive—uncontrolled substitutes.

Shifting to substitutes is not possible if price controls are universal—that is, if all prices and wages are controlled and we have what economists call *suppressed inflation,* or *repressed inflation.* This is worse, not better. If only some items are subjected to price controls, the possibility of spending the remaining money on other items is a kind of safety valve. The uncontrolled items can become extremely expensive, and the excess spending can be drawn off from the economy through taxation of the items or through high taxation of the large profits that may be earned by those who sell them.

Resentment at these very high profits is often responsible for the spread of price controls to uncontrolled items, even when they are goods that could be left only for the rich to purchase and not goods that must be made available to everybody. The spreading of price controls is one way in which particular or selective price controls can become general or even universal price controls.

Universal price controls prevent excess demand from being siphoned off in the purchase of expensive luxury items, and the pressure of the unspent money becomes greater. With nothing left for the money to buy, it is harder than ever to prevent the emergence of black markets, and they come to exist in almost all commodities. Then the most harmful effect is no longer the deprivation of the poor. At this stage in the development of price controls, the more urgent necessities will already be rationed more or less efficiently, so that limited amounts are distributed more reasonably. Black markets will consist of luxuries—items that are not considered worth rationing because they are not necessities.

social disruption

The high black market prices charged for some luxury items arouse great resentment, because these luxuries look just like necessities. They consist of *additional quantities* of the necessities that are being rationed, and this is especially disturbing to those who complain about the meagerness of their rations. But there is really nothing worse about a rich man being able to buy more of something that is made available in limited quantities to everybody at a low price, than it is for him to be able to buy something that looks quite different and that the poor man is used to doing without. Luxuries are by definition too expensive and not particularly necessary—just like additional quantities of necessities. More harmful to society than the actual enjoyment of these black market luxuries by the rich, whether they look like natural luxuries or like more of some rationed "necessity," is the resentments that are generated. These are felt more strongly when they are not seen merely as the difference between being rich and being poor but as the use of the illegal black market to frustrate the rationing system.

Much more serious than either of these resentments is the disrespect for the law that results when wholesale violations become accepted as normal. The development of an attitude of toleration for breaking some laws easily spreads to a tolerance for breaking other laws. Attempts to bolster respect by invoking legal penalties against the transgressors become impossible for the courts to process. Time is taken up with these cases that should be devoted to much more serious crimes. It becomes increasingly difficult for juries to convict offenders who are brought to court and for judges to sentence them, if it is known that hundreds of thousands or even millions of others are equally guilty but unapprehended. The habit of disregarding these offenses—which is bound to develop in such circumstances—spreads to other offenses that are more or less related to the tolerated ones. More serious crimes also become increasingly difficult to punish. They, too, tend to be dealt with more and more leniently or to become practically unpunishable altogether.

Still worse things follow. On the one hand, the failure of the courts to operate results in an increase of crime, as more and more people discover that crime does pay. On the other hand, when conscientious law officers find that the criminals they apprehend with great difficulty and danger are able to circumvent the law, or when the officers consider the punishments inadequate and ineffective, there is a strong temptation for them to take the law into their own hands and to punish the criminals whom the courts cannot, will not, or, in any case, do not punish. This, of course, is not only "police brutality"; it also shows a contempt for the law on the part of those whose duty is to uphold it. It leads, in vicious circles, to a much higher order of disrespect of and disregard for the law.

These are some of the results that are at least encouraged by consistent attempts at universal price control, even if this is not the sole source of such developments in our society. And unfortunately, the authors do not feel this is an exaggeration.

All of these frightening effects have been understood by economists and policy makers for a long time. Nonetheless, controls have often been resorted to because the government's limited taxing abilities prevented it from keeping total spending in the economy from becoming excessive. Governments increased the supply of credit money and created excess demand to increase revenues for defense or to undertake some other "compelling" project. Raising taxes was impossible. The only other available means of generating the necessary revenue was to increase the money supply. Keynes, for example, suggested a combination of higher taxes, wage and price controls, and increases in the money supply as the best way of paying for World War II. In such cases, although the effects of the controls were understood, they were considered to be less harmful than the alternatives—such as being unable to defend the country from foreign invasion. But, in general, economists and regulators hoped for a better way.

incomes policy

That "better way" was an "incomes policy." An incomes policy differs from a controls policy in that it is designed to work *with* the market, not against it. An incomes policy attempts to achieve two objectives: (1) to stabilize the *average* price (or at least to limit its rate of increase to some norm), and at the same time, (2) to allow specific prices and wages to adjust *relatively* to each other, as required by the continually changing tastes, techniques, and availabilities. Such a policy attempts to change relative wages and prices by regulation in the same way that the market would have changed them if the inflation had been less severe—or completely absent.

But this advance is insufficient. Within any system of regulatory controls, someone is bound to feel unfairly treated. In the United States, that "someone" was Labor.

The key part of postwar anti-inflation incomes policies was the "wage guideline," which attempted to keep the increase in wages equal to the average increase in productivity in the economy. Early definitions of wage guidelines were made by Gerhard Colm (1948) and Abba P. Lerner (1951). Over time, the guidelines became progressively refined.

Essentially, these guidelines were statements about the way the economy was supposed to work. Prices in high productivity sectors were supposed to fall, and labor markets were supposed to equilibrate at levels that reflected the skill differentials among workers. Since skill differentials change slowly over time, the wage guidelines should provide rough indicators of the appropriate increase.

Unfortunately, the economy did not work that way, and the productivity guidelines had negative rather than positive effects. They tended to set a floor on wage settlements: The guideline became a minimum rather than an average for wage increases. In addition, prices adjusted too slowly. Labor, in firms that had experienced large technological changes, saw these businesses make large increases in profits while their wage increases were limited to the guideline. This they viewed as inequitable. The problem was that although competition worked, it only worked slowly. In the meantime, labor suffered under wage controls while prices continued to rise. This inevitably broke the controls.

The next logical step in the development of wage guidelines was not taken. This step would have been not to use *labor* productivity but *total productivity* as the benchmark figure. Each firm would then be permitted to make a guideline increase in its Net Sales per unit of input. This development would eliminate the inequity to labor and thus make the guidelines politically more acceptable. MAP essentially incorporates the total productivity concept, and we see it as the natural progression of the earlier concept of a labor productivity guideline.

But even this advance would not be sufficient. Regulatory incomes policies inevitably fail, unless we want to change the total structure of our economy from what is essentially a market economy modified by government to a command and control economy modified by the market, as exists in Russia or China today. The reason incomes policies fail is that they are designed to remake decisions that have already been determined by the market. This is something like having a jury decide whether a baseball umpire has made a fair or an unfair ruling each time a ball or a strike is called, with the jury evenly split between ardent supporters of both teams.

The market serves an *informational* function, *signaling* when and where shortages exist or are expected to arise. The government then does not need to process the indigestible mass of information about all the contributory factors or to undertake all the research that would be necessary to make decisions about these factors. If the government makes these decisions anyway, then the market will not be able to function. This does not mean that the government cannot *influence* the decisions. It can and it should. But to maintain the market system, these decisions must be made by applying a method consistent with the market—that is by changing the property rights, the rules of market interaction, or the tax structure. Regulatory incomes policies follow none of these methods and therefore are inconsistent with the market system and interfere with its operation.

TIP—the use of a price mechanism

A great step forward was taken when suggestions were made to use taxes to control inflation. Wallich and Weintraub's *Tax Based Incomes Policy* (TIP) is the best known in the United States. Their proposal calls for tax incentives (to discourage wage increases) in the form of corporate income surtaxes that would be triggered automatically by the granting of wage increases in excess of some "norm." TIP does not apply to prices, but it relies on the average level of prices continuing to maintain the same proportion in relation to the average level of wages that has been maintained for a very long time by a stable average degree of competition (or degree of imperfection of competition, or degree of monopoly). The surtaxes would hold down wage and price increases and cure—or at least moderate—the inflation. In this way, the incentives would *work through* the market rather than *supplant* the market.

Wallich and Weintraub's original formulation of TIP had some conceptual flaws. One was the use of the analogy of laws against speeding—laws that people can break if they are prepared to pay the fine. This analogy is faulty because a speeding law that kept every driver below the speed limit would be regarded as successful, but a TIP that prevented any wage from rising above the norm would still fail to bring about the desired adjustments in *relative* wages. TIP should be compared to a law—if it can be called a law—that can and should be broken half of the time.

TIP would discourage inflationary wage increases (and therefore also inflationary price increases) by providing an incentive to resist them (in addition to the existing reluctance to pay the increased wage)—all without any suggestion of wrongdoing on the part of anyone who grants wage increases, however great, on which the required incentive taxes are paid. This constitutes the essential advantage of TIP over administrative wage and price regulation, which cannot be avoided legally.

Perhaps it would have been better to call the incentive tax a "disincentive tax," but it was definitely misleading to call the discouragement a "penalty." This clearly suggests a punishment for wrongdoing, and it is probably responsible for the proposal of a more severe punishment for more severe crimes in the form of a *progressive* tax—a more than proportional "penalty" for granting larger wage increases.

Much more serious is the implication that only *excessive* wage increases—increases greater than the norm—are inflationary. The speeding law turns out to be only too close an analogy to TIP's initial suggestion of taxing only firms with average wage increases greater than the norm. In an inflation, it is wage increases *in general* (and price increases *in general*) that are excessive. With changes in tastes, techniques, and availabilities, some wages will rise more than the average and some less. In a general inflation, *all* wage increases need to be reduced. This includes not only wage increases that are less than the norm, but even zero and negative wage increases—wages that are not increasing at all or wages that are actually decreasing. These wages must decline more. *All* wage increases must be discouraged and all wage decreases must be encouraged for exactly the same reason and in exactly the same degree.

It is important to recognize that equal degrees of *disincentive* to raise wages (and of incentive to lower wages) does not mean that *responses* must be equal. Firms must be free to set their own wages (and their own wage increases or decreases)—responding in *different* degree to the uniform disincentive, just as different consumers respond in different degree when they adjust their purchases of a good in response to a uniform change in its price.

Another flaw in the initial TIP proposal was setting the disincentive tax, which varied with the excess wage increases, as a percentage of the firm's profits. This made the disincentive dependent on the profits of the firm (for example, zero incentive for a firm with zero profits).

more efficient TIPs

Larry Seidman, (1976a,b) among others, has suggested improvements to make the disincentive tax (on "excessive" wage increases) *proportional* to the excess wage increase and therefore independent of the profits of the firm. Additional disincentives have also been suggested to discourage below-norm wage increases. (Unfortunately, these are weaker than the disincentives applicable to above-norm wage increases.) These improvements make the disincentive more like a nondiscriminating price. The disincentive tax is essentially a price paid for granting wage increases, so that the total disincentive tax paid by different firms is proportional to the total amount of wage increases (minus the total amount of wage decreases) granted.

Disincentives to discourage below-norm wage increases (by a subsidy that is *reduced* by wage increases) were also suggested by economists, who called them "carrots" instead of "sticks." A TIP that was perfectly adjusted to provide equal disincentives at all levels for equal wage increases—and the same *reverse* (positive) incentives for equal wage reductions—would be an "efficient" TIP. It would work just like a price and would completely solve the incentive problem.

half the market mechanism is missing

But even an "efficient" TIP that applied the same degree of disincentive to all wage increases (and an equal incentive to all wage decreases) would still leave us with the problem of deciding at what level to set these charges and subsidies. It would not solve the problem of deciding *how strong* to make the tax disincentive. Thus, TIP corrects only a part of the flaw. It mobilizes the essential functions of *price* in the price and market mechanism, but not the other half of the price and market mechanism. Still missing is the *market mechanism,* which is needed to set the proper *strength* of the disincentive—the proper *level* of the price or charge that constitutes the disincentive.[1]

an early theoretical market plan

In a seminar on the Integration of the Social Sciences at the New School for Social Research in New York in the late 1940s, Abba P. Lerner developed a purely theoretical plan for dealing with inflation. The plan consisted of an artificial labor market mechanism of maximum simplicity—perhaps we should say crudity—that would mechanically adjust the wage rate in each labor market according to the degree of unemployment in that labor market. It would raise the wage more where the unemployment is much below the national average and raise the wage less where the unemployment is much above the national average, so that the *average* wage increase would be held at just 3 percent per annum (the then estimated national average rate of increase in output per person, or "productivity"). The theoretical plan died of semantic trouble with the sociologists in the seminar.

Lerner later argued for the adoption of his plan as a cure for "administered inflation." The "Lerner Plan" (though not dignified by such a title) was laid to rest in Lerner's *Economics of Employment* (1951) and reinterred in his *Flation* (1972).

The Lerner Plan concentrated entirely on *wage rates,* leaving it to the market to continue to maintain the stable ratio of the average price level to the average wage level. This ratio had been maintained for a long time by a relatively constant degree of competition (or its inverse, the degree of monopoly) between firms and industries, and there was no reason to expect the degree of competition/monopoly to change. The artificial automatic market mechanism was very crude. It could distinguish only three levels of excess supply (levels of unemployment) in labor markets: less than half the national average, more than twice the national average, and anywhere in between. And it could set only three corresponding levels of response in the rates of wage increases: 3 percent annually for the middle range, 6 percent for the very low unemployment labor markets, and zero for the very high unemployment labor markets—or 1 percent, 2 percent, and zero, respectively, three times a year. Continued operation of the "Lerner Plan" could nevertheless provide the relative wage adjustment required. It could keep the average wage rising at 3 percent a year and keep the average price constant while relative wages (gradually) adjusted to changes in relative preferences, techniques, and availabilities.

---

[1] The function of price is to *discourage* whatever activity calls for a price to be *paid* and to *encourage* whatever activity enables a price to be *received.* The function of the market mechanism is to *set the price* at the level that makes the supply equal to the demand.

complete market plans

During the last few years, Lerner developed and refined an alternative plan—WIPP, the Wage Increase Permit Plan (1978). The artificial price mechanism of the old "Lerner Plan" automatically set different wage increases according to only three ranges of unemployment in the different labor markets. WIPP differed from the "Lerner Plan" in four ways.

(1) WIPP made full use of the labor market, including its complex arrangements for individual and collective bargaining and the safeguards and restrictions we have developed here.
(2) It continuously and automatically *monitored* the inflationary pressure.
(3) It automatically *set the incentive* at the level required to offset the inflationary pressure.
(4) It continuously *adjusted* this incentive to changing inflationary pressure.

WIPP, however, shares a fatal difficulty with the early "Lerner Plan" and with most variants of TIP. WIPP concentrates on wages and allows the degree of competition/monopoly in the market to set the normal profit relationship of prices above cost, thereby setting the normal ratio between wages and profits above cost as well. This gives at least an impression of bias against labor—namely of putting all the blame on labor for the tripartite vicious circle of the inflationary process. Thus, all of these plans are unacceptable to labor and therefore are impossible to apply in a democratic society.

At the same time that Lerner was working on WIPP, other market proposals were being developed, including David C. Colander's Free Market Solution to Inflation (FMS), which also employed the market mechanism and its analogue—the "Value Added TIP."

MAP—the Market Anti-inflation Accounting Plan—is the merging of WIPP, the FMS, and the "Value Added TIP."

5

the road to MAP

So far, we have discussed the nature and the cause of inflation and past attempts to control inflation. In this chapter, we will integrate these earlier discussions and demonstrate how they naturally lead to MAP.

Earlier, we distinguished between excess demand inflation and expectational inflation. The former can occur only when the economy is fully extended and total spending is more than enough to buy all that the economy can produce. Excess demand inflation can properly be described as "too much money chasing too few goods," and it can be cured by removing the excess demand. Expectational inflation, which we have been enduring for some time now, occurs when total spending is insufficient to buy all that the economy can produce, but the price level nevertheless continues to rise.

This brief account may give the impression that a sharp line can always be drawn between demand inflation ("too much money chasing too few goods") and expectational inflation (if there are "too few goods," it is only because there is *"not enough money* chasing them," so that it does not pay to produce more). But there is, in fact, no such sharp dividing line. As is the case almost everywhere, the dividing line softens and spreads out over a considerable range. There is a range in which we can have excess demand *with* expectational inflation.

The vagueness arises because full employment is a variable number. As long as there is some uncertainty about future needs or supplies, some *spare capacity* is desirable—not only in the form of unused equipment, but also in the form of unused manpower to work with the unused equipment. And there can be too little as well as too much unused or spare capacity. Too little spare capacity (too high a level of output and employment) results in frequent shortages and disruptions of production and consumption and leaves society in worse shape than it would be with a less full utilization of capacity.

Improvements in its organization or structure can enable the economy to manage as well with less unused capacity—and, consequently, with greater employment and output—but for any given state of the organization, there is a *range* of possible degrees of unused capacity (including unemployment). We can choose between utilizing our resources more fully when things are going smoothly and providing more slack to deal with unanticipated shortages. Views differ as to what compromise we should call "full employment."

Apart from this, another difficulty can confuse us about the kind of inflation we have. An inflation may originate in the purest possible way from a governmental excess spending policy (or for any other reason), yet if it continues for some time, it will *establish* expectations of continuing inflation. An *expectational* race will then be run by wages, prices, and government spending that will persist even if whatever caused the inflation in the first place has disappeared. Any attempted restraint in the rate of increase in total spending below the requirements of the established expectations can check the inflation only by inducing enough *unemployment* to persuade labor to moderate its wage demands. As soon as the spending *ceases to increase more rapidly than is required* to ratify the expected rate of price increase (while maintaining full employment), the inflation becomes pure expectational inflation.

Later in this book, when we consider some of the less obvious problems MAP poses, we will examine more fully what happens to MAP when there is continuing excessive total spending or an institutional inflationary bias. For now, we will limit ourselves to the consideration and treatment of expectational inflation.

faulty social accounting

The flaw that makes wages and prices rise in the futile inflationary race, in which they must run fast to keep up with each other, is a *social* flaw in *private* accounting practices. Just as environmental impacts, health impacts, and other socially important consequences often are not taken into account fully by the individuals and firms making the decisions, the inflationary impacts of wage and price decisions on the economy are not taken into account.

Restrictive monetary and fiscal policy (the appropriate medicine for demand inflation) fails because monetary and fiscal policy attacks this flaw only indirectly through the creation of *unemployment.* The unemployment is intended to offset the inflationary pressures on prices and wages, and therefore on money costs and money prices. But long before the desired effect on prices can be reached via this route, the unemployment becomes too severe, too painful, and too dangerous politically for the treatment to continue. Total spending is then increased—or is permitted to increase—to avoid a catastrophic depression, and the inflation sails on unabated. This leads to fears of escalating inflation—even runaway inflation—and to a desperate resort to wage and price regulation.

Wage and price regulation attacks the flaw directly, but it fails for another reason. Freezing all wages and prices prevents our economic market mechanism from adjusting to continually changing tastes, techniques, and availabilities. Wage and price regulation—permitting wage and price changes subject to bureaucratic approval—is an attempt to provide the necessary noninflationary wage and price adjustments by *administrative* measures. It permits government officials to pass judgment on individual wage and price changes on the basis of inevitably unclear guidelines or guideposts. Attempting to determine all wages and prices in this manner leads to an administrative nightmare and to the abandonment of wage and price regulation.

The only alternative to the abandonment of wage and price regulation (other than the unfeasible spending restraint and deep depression) seems to be to allow them to build a complete bureaucratic, administrative command economy into the price and market economy. These two disparate methods of running the economy cannot be grafted together. But to achieve complete administrative regulation of all wages and prices, we would have to relinquish the entire free enterprise market system.

Fortunately, it is possible to correct the flaw in our price and market mechanism that is responsible for expectational inflation and thereby enable economic policies to succeed in providing economic prosperity with price stability in a free market economy. The central feature of MAP is its concentration on correcting this flaw. But there are a number of other conditions that have to be satisfied at the same time if MAP is to provide a framework for a practical solution to expectational inflation.

the essential ingredients of a solution to inflation

The primary objectives are:

(1)   To keep the *average price* stable.
(2)   To leave all *actual prices flexible,* operating as free market prices at which everybody is able to buy or to sell as much or as little as he or she wishes. The prices must therefore be permitted to rise or fall freely to equalize the demand for each item with its supply. There can be no externally imposed controls on price or on quantity. This will prevent gluts or shortages and the development of black or gray markets. (Monopolistic influence on price through the restriction of output constitutes a serious economic problem, but there is no essential connection between this problem and the problem of inflation.)

The history of anti-inflation policies and their troubles suggests five essential conditions for the satisfactory achievement of these objectives in a democratic, free market society.

(1)   A *counter-inflationary disincentive must be created* to offset the inflationary pressure on prices from the inflationary expectations. This disincentive must be applied at the point at which the prices are determined, namely on the individual firms in the economy.
(2)   *The disincentive must be of just the right strength* to offset the inflationary pressure and to keep the average price (the price level) constant.
(3)   *The disincentive must continuously adjust* to changes in the inflationary pressure. This pressure is bound to change, apart from all

other reasons, because of the operation of the disincentive itself.

(4) *The plan must be seen as fair.* The plan must not discriminate between different prices or between business and labor. This means that the disincentive must apply in the same strength to *all* prices, because in an inflation all prices tend to rise relative to what their level would have been in the absence of inflation. The disincentive must not intervene in the division of income between profits and wages, which should be left to the existing system of individual or collective free bargaining.

It is tempting to say that the plan should *be fair* before saying that it must be *seen to be fair,* but the latter is the more fundamental proposition. The first statement sounds much more basic, but it only means that it seems fair *to us, too.*

Fairness has often been claimed by other anti-inflation plans in the form of a request for equal *sacrifice*—for everybody to tighten his or her belt equally. We enthusiastically agree with the desirability of fairness, but we see no need for sacrifice or belt-tightening. On the contrary, as the monetary-fiscal restraint that is responsible for the stagflation becomes unnecessary, we may be able to move toward fuller employment and output. It is the sharing of these *benefits* that must be fair.

The uniform application of the same disincentive to all prices does not mean that there will be a uniform *adjustment* of the price or the quantity of the item traded. Nor does it prevent the differential application of other incentives or disincentives for other purposes.

(5) *The plan must be simple* enough to be administratively feasible and to be understood and accepted by the general public. Thus, it must not take too long to show results. The simplicity condition requires that while the disincentive must work on *all* wages and prices, there should be no special limitations on the behavior of specific prices or specific wage rates.

None of the solutions proposed until now have satisfied all five conditions. Monetary-fiscal policy alone, operating only through depression and unemployment, concentrates a special burden on the unemployed and fails on fairness. Regulatory guideposts fail on *flexibility,* on *fairness,* and on *feasibility.* The essence of the market and price mechanism is that reasonable decisions can be made by a firm without knowledge of all the relative prices that would make the economy operate efficiently, but only with a knowledge of what *that particular* firm must do to adjust to the actual prices at which it can buy and sell.

But wage and price regulators have to agree on relative prices, and policy makers throughout history have been unable to determine what the proper set of relative prices are. They have neither the experience nor the data to make these decisions; it is actually impossible for anyone to collect all the required information.

Wage and price regulators therefore continually try to avoid or to postpone making a decision. When they are finally forced to decide, their decision reflects not the change in price that is economically warranted, but the one that is politically feasible. Such considerations as "demonstration effects" prevail.

These results are inevitable when the weapons for bringing about compliance are prosecution under antitrust laws, decisions about the disposition of government stockpiles of strategic materials, or the awarding of government contracts—with a final appeal for public demonstrations.

It is also generally conceded, even by their supporters, that wage-price guidelines have not been fair. It is essential that these guidelines should be considered fair by almost everybody, because without social consensus no anti-inflation action is possible. It must be accepted, at least passively, by all the major groups that it will affect.

The issue of uniform treatment of all *prices* is really more a matter of economic efficiency than of fairness. Fairness is much more basic in the treatment of the rewards offered to different *people*. This is most conspicuous in the division of income between wages and profits. With far too many prices to control, wages—being easier to control than prices—have been singled out in almost all proposals for stronger enforcement measures. In the Nixon controls, this unequal treatment prompted labor to walk off the Wage Board.

Attempts to meet the charge of inequity toward labor result either in guarantees that cannot be fulfilled or in unfairness toward business. But if profits are limited, investment will be reduced, resulting in negative effects on productivity and growth. A good example of guarantees that could not be fulfilled is the promise the British government extended to labor in the early 1970s. To secure labor's support of its incomes policy, the government guaranteed labor a certain real income. When OPEC unexpectedly raised the price of oil, real income in Britain had to decrease. Since labor had been guaranteed its real income, the government found itself in an untenable bind. The results counsel strongly against such guarantees in the United States. Similarly, we can say with some confidence that the 1979 guideposts will also collapse because of their inequities.

We have listed five essential conditions for a successful plan to cure our expectational inflation and have shown how the two policies for dealing with inflation that were actually attempted—monetary-fiscal restraint and wage-price controls—have failed to satisfy these conditions. A number of incentive plans that have been proposed in recent years satisfy more of the conditions—but not all of them. In designing MAP to satisfy all five conditions, we have gained very much from our study of the advantages and disadvantages of the incentive plans, a number of which will be examined in Chapter 11.

In Chapter 6, we will spell out a simple application of the MAP framework to illustrate the mechanism that satisfies these conditions. We will then examine the following benefits that emerge from MAP in addition to the ones we have already singled out as essential conditions.

(1)   The successful implementation of MAP depends on the simultaneous successful maintenance of a sound monetary-fiscal policy by the gov-

ernment (a policy that supplies neither too much nor too little total spending in the economy to provide a satisfactory level of employment at the current price level). Excessive total spending would cause MAP to break down, and deficient total spending would cause a depression that would (unjustly) discredit and destroy MAP. But MAP provides a *guide* that makes it much easier for the government to carry out the required sound monetary-fiscal policy. *This policy is "sound," not because it is what keeps prices stable, but because it is appropriate if some independent policy (like MAP) is keeping the price level constant.*

(2) Keeping the price level constant permits total income—both total wages and total profits—to rise with the increase in the productivity of labor and capital services as well as with the increase in their supply. MAP provides automatic adjustments for both of these increases without dictating the distribution of the product between wages and profits. It does this by applying the counter-inflationary disincentive not to wages alone and not to profits alone but to the *combination* of the two in each firm's *Net Sales*. In this way, MAP avoids even appearing to be biased toward labor or capital. A slight adjustment to Net Sales for government (and other nonprofit) enterprises also permits MAP to treat private and public enterprises identically.

(3) MAP is *self-deflating.* As MAP proceeds, by its counter-inflationary disincentive, to reduce the rate of inflation, it also reduces the *expectation* of inflation (as the public notices the reduction in the *actual* inflation). This approach—working on the expectation through the actual inflation on which the expectation is built—is the reverse approach to "jawboning," which tries to persuade the public that the inflation is diminishing when it is obviously continuing, or even accelerating.

As the inflationary expectation is reduced, the strength of the disincentive must be reduced correspondingly. MAP provides for an automatic reduction in the disincentive in response to reductions in the expectation of inflation. Thus, in disinflating the inflation, MAP also disinflates its own operation. Unless some inflationary pressures other than the inflationary expectations are operative, the disincentive automatically falls to zero when the inflation is completely overcome. Any distortions that result from the disincentive will then disappear as MAP completes its task.

(4) Once MAP has disinflated the inflation and, at the same time, has reduced the strength of the disincentive to zero, the *structure* of MAP will not disappear. It is ready all the time to come into action if any new inflationary movement begins. As soon as any inflationary expectations are created, the disincentive automatically increases and starts checking and eliminating the new inflation. MAP lies *dormant but ready* to start working again immediately if it is ever needed.

(5) MAP also works in reverse, without any change in its structure. If an *expectational deflation* (as occurred in the United States in the 1930s),

when prices fall because people expect them to fall, should ever arise again, MAP will automatically produce a *counter-deflationary disincentive* that makes price *de*creases more expensive in exactly the same way that the counter-*in*flationary disincentive makes price *in*creases more expensive. Some recognition of the need for a mechanism such as MAP to cure the expectational deflation of the 1930s was shown by attempts at the time to induce price increases by such measures as raising the price of gold and stimulating monopolies under the National Recovery Act of the New Deal. Although these measures were not helpful, they did indicate a glimmering of the recognition of the need for something to arrest the tripartite deflationary spiral in which the economy was then caught.

Despite our claims, we recognize that MAP is not a panacea. MAP, like all other programs, has advantages and disadvantages. The road to MAP will not be easy. However, since all other existing roads to a stable economy are impassable, the road to MAP, although rocky, should be traversed.

the MAP framework

The rules for the operation of the Market Anti-inflation Accounting Plan can be varied in many ways without disrupting its general operation. In this chapter, we will spell out perhaps the simplest possible form of MAP, which we will call Model A. The aim of this model is the *complete* elimination of the inflation in the shortest possible time. The nature of variations that would not interfere with MAP's operation is discussed, and a number of these variations are then examined in Chapter 7.

rules for a Model A MAP

(1) The Federal Reserve is currently responsible for maintaining a sound money supply, which means a money supply *compatible* with price stability and with economic prosperity. To achieve this, price stability and prosperity must be made compatible with each other. The Federal Reserve's responsibility is therefore extended by Congress to include responsibility for the *maintenance of price stability* through MAP.

In an expectational inflation, a "sound money policy" is impossible because prosperity can be maintained only by permitting the money supply and the total spending in the economy to "ratify" the expected rising prices— the "price instability." Only when price stability is being maintained by some other means can a sound monetary policy be carried out.

(2) A Federal Reserve MAP Credit Office credits each firm, at no cost to the firm, with a basic MAP Credit equal to its dollar *Net Sales* in the previous year.

A *firm* is any employer subject to income tax. *Net Sales* is gross sales, including "internal sales" (inventory increases at cost), *minus* purchases from other firms (which are counted in the sales of the other firms). Each firm's Net Sales is therefore equal to its profits *plus* its wages. Net Sales includes interest payments, rents, fees, and other payments that constitute income to individuals, as well as wages, salaries, and the cost of all fringe

39

benefits. National total *Net Sales* is the same as *total spending* on final goods, since somebody must be buying what is being sold. National total Net Sales consists of the total profits and the total wage bill, in the wide senses of these terms. It is the same as *total income,* which an incomes policy, to prevent inflation, must keep growing parallel to the increase in total output.

(3)   Hiring a new employee (including all the employees of a new firm) entitles the firm to additional free MAP Credit from the MAP Credit Office. This Credit is equal to the employee's Wage (including fringe benefits) in his or her *previous* job. Conversely, the separation of an employee from a firm reduces the Credit of the firm by the amount of that employee's Wage. The free Credit must be equal to the previous Wage to prevent firms from firing and rehiring employees at higher salaries to obtain additional free Credit for the difference.

(4)   New capital investment (whether financed by stocks, bonds, or reinvested declared profits, including all the capital investments of a new firm) entitles the firm to additional free Credit equal to interest on the new investment at the interest rate. This represents the payment (Wage) for the services of the new capital. Conversely, the retirement of invested capital correspondingly reduces a firm's MAP Credit.

If a firm buys another firm, there is no net investment in the economy. Additional MAP Credit is granted only on the *value of increases* in capital invested and not on *increases in the value* of capital already invested. The buying firm acquires the other firm's stock of MAP Credit, together with its other assets.

(5)   The MAP Credit Office grants each firm a further increase in free Credit, equal to 2 percent per annum of its total Credit, to allow for the estimated national average growth of net output per unit of input. The purpose of the 2 percent annual increase in each firm's free Credit is only to keep the national *average* increase in Net Sales per unit of input at just 2 percent.

(6)   All firms are required to keep their Net Sales and their MAP Credit equal to each other by buying or selling Credit or by increasing or decreasing their Net Sales. The latter must be achieved by increasing or decreasing their prices, *not* by changing their inputs.

To facilitate this, the MAP Credit Office maintains a market in MAP Credit, buying or selling this Credit freely to all comers and adjusting the price to keep supply and demand equal. The demand for Credit comes from "deficit" firms who are short of Credit (their Net Sales exceeds their Credit). The supply of MAP Credit comes from "surplus" firms (their Credit exceeds their Net Sales). No MAP Credit is created or destroyed in this trade, so that the total amount of MAP Credit in the economy remains unchanged.

Any firm that increases its Net Sales per unit of input by more than 2 percent is charging *more* than the national average increase in the value of output per unit of input. This may take the form of an increase in the *price* per unit of output, or in an increase in the *output* per unit of input, or in some combination of the two. In all cases, the greater increase in Net Sales per unit of input is presumably warranted by a greater-than-average scarcity of the product. But if inflation is to be prevented, this must be balanced by opposite deviations elsewhere that result in *less-than-average* increases in Net Sales per unit of input, due to a less-than-average scarcity of the product. Opposite deviations occur in the "surplus" firms, where Net Sales per unit of input increases by less than 2 percent (or actually decreases).

Increases or decreases in a firm's Net Sales due only to changes in its scale of operation will be accompanied by proportional changes in the inputs that provide a proportional change in the firm's free Credit. Net Sales and the firm's total Credit will therefore increase or decrease together, and the firm will not need to buy or sell MAP Credit.

As a result of all these provisions, the total national volume of Credit will increase in proportion to the total national increase in productive resources *plus* the (estimated) national increase in net output per unit of productive resources. This means that total Net Sales (kept equal to total Credit) will grow at the same rate as total net output. Thus, the average price—the price level—will not change.

Since MAP Credit is freely tradable, it can also be acquired for a temporary period to match a temporary increase in the firm's Net Sales by buying MAP Credit to sell later. Conversely, MAP Credit can be sold to match a temporary reduction in Net Sales. The same effects might be achieved more conveniently by *renting* some MAP Credit for the period. But to simplify the exposition, we will speak only of buying and selling MAP Credit, even though the sole operative requirement is that the firm *be in possession* of an amount of MAP Credit equal to its Net Sales over the period (the year) during which Net Sales occur.

(7) The MAP Credit Office keeps a record of each firm's Credit as it is adjusted for hirings and separations of employees, changes in capital investments, and purchases and sales of Credit, to check whether the Credit in the firm's possession matches its Net Sales. Such records are required by the Internal Revenue Service or by the Social Security Administration with which the MAP Credit Office would cooperate. The maintenance of these records is no more "mind boggling" than the task currently being handled by Master Charge computers.

(8) Government agencies and private nonprofit corporations are also subject to MAP regulations. In these cases, "Net Sales" is replaced by "Net Personal Income Generated" (the nonprofit part of Net Sales). Thus, business and government are both treated the same way.

what MAP does *not* do

We have just reviewed the basic rules for the operation of MAP. We must now examine them in much greater detail to clarify the manner in which the rules are to be carried out. We will deal with some of these details when we consider possible variations of MAP in Chapter 7. However, it does seem to be almost as necessary to list some of the things that MAP does *not* do as to list the things that it does do.

MAP does not cure the common cold, and there are many other individual and social problems that it does not help to solve. It merely cures inflation.

MAP does not provide any instructions, permission, or even advice as to what wages or prices to set or what quantities of any items to buy or to sell, other than to require that each firm adjust its Credit to its Net Sales or its Net Sales to its Credit.

MAP does not regulate wages or prices. MAP *audits* the records of a firm (in the same way an audit is conducted for income tax purposes) to see that its claimed Credit holding is based on true information about its previous Net Sales, its hirings and firings of employees, its Wages, and its increases or decreases in capital invested in the firm. Undoubtedly, there would be temptations to misrepresent these data, but they would probably be far less powerful than the temptations to cheat on income taxes and offenders could be dealt with in the same way. Raising prices, and thereby Net Sales, is completely legitimized by the purchase of Credit, but failing to purchase the legitimizing Credit or falsely reporting the purchase of such Credit is equivalent to cheating on income tax reports.

Since MAP Credit is an entirely new commodity to be put on the market, some unanticipated difficulties may arise. But it is a perfectly simple, homogeneous commodity that presents no problems of quality estimation. There are no brand differences, no transportation problems, and no dangers that MAP Credit will become decayed, spoiled, or out of fashion. There is no need for any quality control. Only the *strangeness* of MAP must be overcome, and there is no reason for this market to be any more difficult to operate or any less perfect than, say, the market in shares of IBM.

no free MAP credit
for increased relative productivity

No allowance of additional MAP Credit is made for the *particular* increase in the productivity of a firm or an industry. To provide increases in Credit for firms that exhibit an above-average increase in productivity would result in irresistible demands for identical increases from other equally deserving producers who have not been lucky enough to benefit from a particular technological advance. But any above-average increases must be balanced by *below-average* increases in Credit elsewhere if total Net Sales are to be kept from increasing relative to total net output. A firm that increases its output per worker from increased investment or that increases its output per unit of invested capital from the use of more manpower is, of course, granted increased Credit for these increased inputs of capital or manpower.

MAP alone is not enough

By concentrating on Net Sales, which covers both prices and wages, MAP deals with only *two* of the three elements in the tripartite race between wages, prices, and total spending in the expectational inflationary process. It remains necessary for the government to adjust the level of spending to prevent too much spending (which would result in a demand inflation) or too little spending (which would result in a depression). Without a sound finance policy that prohibits excessive as well as deficient total money supply and total spending, MAP will not be able to perform its task. It is important, however, to realize that the reverse is also true. Without the stabilization of the price level that MAP would achieve, the authorities cannot implement a sound finance policy. Only the *combination* of a price stabilization plan with a sound finance policy can produce the desired result.

the price of MAP credit

MAP is an *incentive* plan. It provides a disincentive that induces firms to hold down their Net Sales relative to their inputs of labor and capital services. The disincentive consists of the price of the Credit, which is determined by the demand for and the supply of Credit by firms. The price of Credit is automatically adjusted by the market, so that it is always equal to the inflationary pressure it is designed to overcome. The greater the expectation of price increases (the more virulent the expectational inflation), the more will firms offer to pay for additional Credit to permit them to charge higher prices to increase their Net Sales—and the less willing will suppliers of Credit be to sell it to them. Thus, firms will have to lower their prices to keep *their* Net Sales down. The price of Credit will then be high. This will discourage firms from raising their prices (and their Net Sales) and will compel them to buy additional expensive Credit. It will also encourage firms to lower their prices (and their Net Sales), enabling them to sell valuable Credit, until the supply becomes equal to the demand.

As long as the supply is less than the demand, the price of MAP Credit will rise higher and higher until the equality between supply and demand is reached. This is how MAP automatically sets the disincentive (the price of MAP Credit) at the right strength—just equal to the inflationary pressure—so that the average price neither rises nor falls.

MAP attacks inflation directly

Much, if not all, of the inflationary pressure—the pressure that raises the wages and prices that constitute Net Sales—is generated by inflationary *expectations.* MAP has no direct effect on these expectations. It is impossible to destroy or even to weaken the inflationary expectations as long as the inflation itself continues, because the observation of the on-going inflation creates and maintains the inflationary expectations. MAP stops the *actual* inflation and counts on the observation of the disappearance of the inflation to reduce the inflationary expectations.

how long would MAP take?

To see how MAP would work, we will consider a very simple example— beginning with a state of affairs that does not differ greatly from what we have been experiencing in actuality for some time—and determine how long MAP should take to cure the inflation.

We will assume that MAP is put into force when an expectational inflation has been going on for some time. During this period, prices have risen 6 percent per annum, labor and capital inputs have increased at a rate of 2 percent, and productivity has increased at a rate of 2 percent. Total Net Sales (which is identical to total spending and to the total of wages plus profits) has therefore been increasing at 10 percent per annum. This is outlined in Table 1.

table 1

Annual rates of increase of:

The Price Level	Total Inputs	Output per Unit of Input	Total Real Output	Total Value Added Total Net Sales Total Net Income Wages + Profits
6%	2%	2%	4%	10%

Since prices have been rising and are expected to continue to rise, there will be a demand for additional Credit to legitimize the 10 percent increase in Net Sales from the expected 6 percent increase in prices. The price of Credit will be correspondingly high. But as it becomes apparent that the *actual* average increase in Net Sales is only 4 percent, the 10 percent expectation will diminish and so will the demand for extra Credit. The price of Credit will consequently fall.

Any continuing expectation of *any* inflation at all, which depends on Net Sales increasing at some rate *greater than* 4 percent, is bound to be disappointed and revised downward. When the inflationary expectations have been completely eliminated by the disappointments, the expectational inflation will be cured. There will be no expectational inflation and no demand for Credit, and its price will fall to zero—or to whatever price may be necessary to offset any institutional upward push on prices.

As with any other anti-inflation plan, firms may be tempted to try to beat the gun and qualify for a larger base Credit by establishing higher base Net Sales. If they succeed, a pre-MAP spurt in the inflation could result. But this could be prevented by granting the base Credit on Net Sales during some period before the actual introduction of MAP was anticipated. Once MAP is installed, the goal of price stability will be reached as soon as the rules are understood and obeyed. If, as seems pretty certain, there is a lively prior discussion, the cure could take very little time, no time at all, or even *less than no time!*

Without a general expectation that the inflation will stop or be significantly reduced soon after the imposition of MAP, there is no possibility of applying MAP. After the base Net Sales of firms have been set, such an expectation would lead to the anticipation of smaller future price increases, a greater readiness of sellers to accept lower price increases now rather than wait, and a greater willingness of buyers to wait rather than to buy now. This would result in at least *a slow-down—if not a complete cessation—of the inflation before MAP has become fully operative and has ensured that each firm's Net Sales is equal to the amount of its MAP Credit.* Any remaining expectation of average price increases will meet with quick disappointment and will be reconsidered.

_____ table 2 _____

1	2	3	4	5	6	7
Expected Inflation Rate	6%	6%	6%	6%	3%	0
MAP Credit Price	—	?	$1.00 (max.)	$.50	$.25	0

Firm Groups	Expected Increase (Decrease) in Net Sales and Demand for Extra (Supply of Spare) MAP Credit (As a Percentage of the Firm's Previous Year's Net Sales)					
A	26	22	22	22	19	16
B	20	16	16	16	13	10
C	15	11	11	11	8	5
D	10	6	6	6	3	0
E	5	1	1	1	(2)	(5)
F	0	(4)	(100)*	(4)	(7)	(10)
G	(6)	(12)	(100)*	(52)*	(34)*	(16)
MAP Credit Market		(shortage)	(glut)	(-----------Equilibrium-----------)		

*Total or partial shift from normal selling of output to pathological selling of "inherited" MAP Credit.

the impact of MAP on different firms

The manner in which this disinflation process appears to work in different firms—with different expectations of increases in prices and Net Sales—is illustrated in Table 2. There, groups of firms from A to G are arranged in descending order of their pre-MAP expectations of the increases in their own Net Sales. These expected increases in Net Sales are listed in column 2 as percentages of each firm's Net Sales in the previous year. (Decreases are shown in parentheses.)

Firm D, the central firm (or group of firms), also represents the *average* firm with average expectations, so that its expectation of the increase in its own prices is the same as the general expectation of the increase in the price level. Therefore, firm D can be considered as a "representative firm"—a kind of model of the economy as a whole. Firm D expects its prices to rise at the national average rate of expected price increases, which is 6 percent. It is increasing its input of labor and capital at the national average rate of 2 percent, and it is expecting its productivity to increase at the national average rate of 2 percent. Firm D therefore expects its total real output to increase at 4 percent, which, at the expected price increase of 6 percent, will increase its Net Sales about 10 percent. This is the same percentage cited in Table 1 for the economy as a whole.

Column 3 represents the situation immediately after the imposition of MAP, before previous expectations have been disturbed (before anyone has noticed that the inflation has been stopped). At the risk of giving the impression that MAP will take a long time to work, we make the quite unrealistic assumption that there is no recognition of the effects of MAP for some time. We do this so that we can deal separately with the effects of the recognition. Column 3 lists each firm's demand for extra Credit at 4 percentage points less than the expected percentage increase in Net Sales, because each firm will receive 2 percent additional Credit (on the average) for increased inputs and 2 percent for increased national average productivity. The question mark in column 3 for MAP Credit price indicates that the firms have not yet considered the price of Credit and have merely calculated how much Credit they would have to buy (or sell) on the basis of their previous expectations of Net Sales.

how high will the price of MAP credit be?

Assuming, for simplicity, that each group of firms has the same total volume of previous Net Sales, column 3 of Table 2 shows that the supply of Credit (the sum of the numbers in parentheses) is much less than the demand for Credit (the sum of the remaining numbers). This is indicated by the legend "shortage" at the bottom of column 3. The demand for Credit, without taking price into account, is much greater than the supply. Thus, the price will have to rise above zero. But how high will it rise?

As long as the expected increases in prices of goods and the expected Net Sales remain unchanged, no increase in the price of Credit will be enough. The same unequal numbers for supply and demand will remain.

There are, however, limits to how high the price of Credit will rise. Here, too, the rule also holds that what goes up must come down. The far outside limit to the increase in the rental price of Credit is one dollar per unit per year (which permits a year's Net Sales to increase by one dollar). At this price, all firms that do not expect any increase in their Net Sales would find it profitable to stop selling whatever they were producing and to rent out their MAP Credit! This is also true for firms that could increase their Net Sales but that would profit more by temporarily reducing their Net Sales and renting out some of their Credit. In column 4 of Table 2, the two lowest groups of producers choose this path and offer *all* their Credit, thereby making the supply much greater than the demand. This only indicates that the maximum price of $1.00 would not stand. At that price, there would be a "glut" (as the legend reads) and the price would decrease again.

Column 5 shows a partial equilibrium. At a Credit price of $.50, only the G firms cut down on real output and (together with the F firms) supply enough Credit to satisfy the demand from firms A–E. Thus, there is equilibrium in the MAP Credit market, but we are very far from equilibrium in the economy as a whole. We are still assuming that everybody expects a continuation of the 6 percent inflation—with the corresponding 10 percent increase in total Net Sales on which the individual firms' particular expectations of their Net Sales depend. Meanwhile, *MAP has stopped the actual inflation.* All actual increases in Net Sales have been completely offset by equal actual decreases in the Net Sales of the firms that supplied the Credit necessary to legitimize the increases. We must now begin to consider the effects of the *actual* stoppage of the inflation and of the price of Credit on the behavior of the firms.

partial responses to MAP

In column 6 of Table 2, the lesson has been half learned. There has been a downward revision in the expected or planned Net Sales, corresponding to a decline in the expected inflation rate from 6 percent to 3 percent. But there is still no equilibrium in the economy as a whole.

Columns 4 and 5 describe situations in which only F and G firms respond to the MAP disincentive—the price paid for extra Credit or (in their cases) the price obtained from selling Credit. The high price of Credit was sufficient to induce the F and G firms to *halt or reduce production* and rent out all or part of their Credit. The other firms, who were expanding their Net Sales, rented (or bought) corresponding amounts of extra Credit as if it did not cost anything at all. The extreme responses by the F and G firms are as unrealistic as the nonresponses of the A–E firms.[1]

Column 6 shows the partial reactions of the A–F firms to the recognition that something is happening. This could be the result of a drop in the inflationary expectations from 6 percent to 3 percent (as indicated in Table 2). That would cause the three-point reduction in the expected Net Sales and the three-point reduction in the demand for Credit shown in the table. This activity would mean that firms A–F are giving no consideration at all to the disincentive—to the market price of Credit.

The same reduction in the demand for Credit could also be the result of considering the cost of the Credit. This would make the expected expansion of Net Sales appear less profitable even if inflationary expectations were to remain at 6 percent (contrary to the 3 percent indicated in column 6). A somewhat more reasonable explanation would be some combination of these two conditions—some reduction in the inflationary expectation (the fear of not being able to sell as much at each price) combined with some response to the cost of buying extra Credit. Fortunately, it is not necessary to determine the proportions of the two forces that lead to the reduction in the demand for Credit. MAP can complete its task independently of whether the initial response is due to one, both, or any combination of the two conditions. This is because the two forces begin to merge as awareness of the situation

---

[1] In the unrealistic situation depicted in columns 4 and 5, the prices and Net Sales of firms A–E would continue to increase at the expected rates if the demand for the goods that the F and G firms have stopped producing were transferred to the output produced by firms A–E.

increases. As the inflationary expectation is reduced, so is the demand for Credit, and its price—the counter-inflationary disincentive—is kept equal to the inflationary pressure by the market, which equalizes the total demand for and the total supply of Credit. Both diminish together with the growing recognition that the inflation has come to an end, and the inflationary expectation and the price of Credit both reach zero together.

Column 6 still shows incomplete responses from firms A–F and an excessive response from firm G (although on a smaller scale than indicated in columns 4 and 5). Columns 4–6 show a pathological condition resulting from our artificial but simplistic assumption of initial imperviousness to reductions in actual total Net Sales and to the cost of buying Credit.

equilibrium

Column 7 shows the equilibrium position when the response to the price of Credit (or to the ending of the *actual* inflation) has spread throughout the economy and has reduced the planned Net Sales of all firms to levels compatible with the stabilized total actual Net Sales. At this point, there is now no need for any excessive responses from firms living on their "inherited" Credit.

As long as there is any remaining expectation of inflation—and firms are correspondingly overly optimistic in planning their Net Sales—the need for extra Credit will be greater than the available spare Credit and a positive price will be charged for Credit. The price of Credit will continue to operate as an incentive to firms to reduce all planned Net Sales still further—by encouraging some firms to reduce their expenditures on extra Credit and other firms to increase their revenues from the sale of spare Credit. Equilibrium can be reached only when the inflationary expectation has been completely eliminated and the existing state of stable prices has established an expectation of continuing stable prices. Whether this will take a lot of time, a little time, or "less than no time" (due to the anticipation of the results of MAP) will be known only if and when MAP is put into practice.

stability

The symmetry of the numbers above and below the "average" D firms in column 7 shows the equilibrium between the demand for extra Credit (the numbers above D) and the supply of spare Credit (the numbers in parentheses below D). This equilibrium is the only possible "normal" stable situation in the MAP Credit market (as long as inflationary expectations solely constitute the inflationary pressures[2]). Any positive price of Credit would indicate inflationary expectations, would act as a disincentive to Net Sales, would bring about a *decline* in planned prices and Net Sales, and would correct the inflationary tendency.

---

[2]The possibility that some inflationary pressures other than inflationary expectations would have to be offset will be discussed in Chapter 11.

MAP self-disinflates

This is how MAP, in disinflating the inflation, disinflates the price of Credit— the power of the counter-inflationary disincentive—at the same time. Such a self-disinflation follows naturally from the use of the market mechanism in MAP to set the disincentive at the level that just overcomes the inflationary pressure. As the disincentive diminishes the inflationary pressure by discouraging increases in Net Sales (and encouraging decreases in Net Sales), it must itself diminish in strength if it is to remain equal to the diminishing inflationary pressure. When the disincentive finally accomplishes its task by completely curing the inflation, it will have reduced the inflationary pressure to zero and, consequently, must itself also be reduced to zero.

However, the whole structure of MAP will not have disappeared. The rules will still remain in force. Firms with above-average increases in Net Sales (firms A, B, and C) will still have to buy Credit, and firms with below-average increases in Net Sales (firms E, F, and G) will still have to sell Credit, even though the price of Credit is zero. These exercises keep MAP fit for significant operation if a new inflation ever starts. As soon as any expectation of continuing inflation is generated, there is an excess demand for Credit and the price of Credit becomes positive to equal and offset the inflationary pressure.

A new inflation may not begin as an expectational inflation. Indeed, expectational inflation usually begins with a demand inflation, a cost push inflation, a serious production shortage, or an increase in the prices of important imports. MAP would work in exactly the same way to offset the inflationary pressure, whatever its cause.

Of particular interest is the reaction of MAP to an inflation caused by too much total spending due to governmental fiscal or monetary measures. This is rarely a deliberate policy intended to foment an inflation (although some extreme monetarists make much of the fact that the government not only collects more money in an inflation, like most firms and individuals, but also can buy more resources with the money it creates). Monetary authorities usually do not know whether they are increasing total spending too little or too much. MAP can be of great service in this connection. Any excessive total spending immediately increases Net Sales per unit of input and creates a positive Credit price. Any deficiency in total spending prevents firms, on the average, from reaching their planned Net Sales. They will have some spare Credit to sell, and this will create a negative Credit price. The resulting positive or negative price of Credit will provide a sensitive signal to the authorities, indicating when they are providing too much or too little total spending to achieve prosperity without inflation.

variants
of MAP

In Chapter 5, we presented the central idea of MAP. In Chapter 6, we outlined one method (MAP Model A) of implementing the MAP concept and described some workings of the MAP proposal.

It is the concept of MAP—not the specifics of MAP A—that we believe is essential to finding a solution to inflation. Neither of us possesses the necessary expertise to make the final decision as to precisely how MAP should be organized. As various aspects of the proposal are considered, we expect numerous modifications to be introduced. In this chapter, we will review the specifics of MAP A and some of the many possible modifications of MAP, suggesting some alternative formulations and design characteristics of an ongoing MAP. In Chapter 8, we will consider some of the problems involved in starting up MAP.

operational control and
the mechanics of the market

MAP A delegates operational control to the Federal Reserve System (the FED), for reasons we believe are important. However, if some reasons that we have not considered argue against giving control to the FED, MAP could be regulated by some other government agency, such as the Treasury, the Council on Wage and Price Stability, or the Securities and Exchange Commission. MAP could even be implemented by a private organization, such as a collection of banks. None of these possibilities would substantially alter MAP. Even if it were controlled by the FED, the actual mechanics of buying and selling MAP Credit would probably be conducted through commercial banks or private organizations.

A more fundamental question is how will an "orderly" market be maintained independently of whatever organization or agency is chosen to administer it. In MAP A, the price of MAP Credit is set by the forces of supply and demand. This, of course, still allows some administrative regulation to maintain an "orderly market" and to smooth out the day-to-day fluctuations in the price of MAP Credit, much as is done in the stock market.

As in other markets, it is always possible that speculation could push the price of MAP Credit up to an extremely high level, with the attendant effects on the real economy. This raises the question of whether there should be a stabilization fund of, say, 1 percent of the total MAP Credit, which would allow the government or some other agency to take an active role in influencing the price or "protecting" it from speculators. But a large stabilization fund would endanger the self-regulating nature of the price level under MAP and could introduce many of the same political considerations into MAP that have caused problems with monetary policy.

If destabilizing speculation becomes a significant problem, it may be necessary to limit holdings of MAP Credit to a "reasonable amount" that reflects the firm's potential needs. As is well known in foreign exchange markets, such rules cause administrative problems and should be avoided if possible.

We would expect a forward market in MAP Credit to develop in addition to a number of alternative sales arrangements. One such arrangement would be a repurchase agreement allowing firms to "rent" MAP Credit for temporary fluctuations in Net Sales per unit of input.

Here, again, some rules may be required to limit possible destabilizing speculation. All MAP Credit traded in the market would have to be certified in the same way that options are certified to ensure that the sellers can meet their obligations. Some form of insurance system might be developed for this purpose.

There are, of course, many other possibilities. Although we hope that the MAP Credit market will be kept as simple as possible, we must recognize that actual markets are complicated creatures.

inclusiveness of the program

MAP A was designed for all "firms," including nonprofit and governmental organizations. A number of alternative models of MAP might be considered for administrative reasons. For example, it would be possible to include only firms above a certain size, to be determined by the number of employees hired, net sales, net assets, or some combination of these factors. A minimum figure for Net Sales might be $500,000 or $1,000,000. Making such a blanket exclusion would eliminate many firms for which the calculation of inputs is especially difficult and would consequently avoid considerable accounting problems. On the other hand, it would introduce some inefficiencies as well as provide opportunities to avoid or evade the MAP rules.

As long as the MAP Credit price is not high or the noncovered sector is competitive with the covered sector, limiting the applicability of MAP will not cause serious problems. If such competition is limited, a high MAP Credit price will encourage the reorganization of firms into smaller, noncovered units and will also induce a firm to transfer employees into the noncovered sector for a month, give them a 50 percent raise, and then bring them back into the covered sector to obtain the larger MAP Credit for the "previous wage." Some method of preventing such arrangements would need to be devised, such as extending free MAP Credit only to cover the actual wage paid or an individual's previous wage, whichever is lower.

A variant of MAP might exclude the agricultural sector. This would diminish price stability because the price level would rise and fall with the movement of agricultural prices. Nevertheless, it might be advisable to exclude this sector in order to give the price level some flexibility in response to shifts in agricultural prices. Including the sector would make it necessary for all other prices to fall or rise to offset a rise or fall in agricultural prices. A temporary movement of agricultural prices seems to be a much more efficient method of achieving the same necessary change in real income. A size exclusion, considered earlier, would largely cover this agricultural problem.

Over an extended period, it should make little difference whether truly competitive sectors are included or not. The good years in which firms bought Credit would simply offset the bad years when firms had Credit to sell. Of course, Credit could be priced differently in good and bad years, which might mean that their relative positions would not be the same.

Another variant of MAP might exclude government and nonprofit organizations. However, this would present more serious problems because the fairness of MAP could then be questioned. Government organizations contribute to inflation in the same way that other groups in the private sector do. Under MAP A, if a government department wants to expand its income payments per unit of input, it must offset that contribution to inflation by buying Credit (inducing disinflation on the part of the sellers of the Credit).

statutory responsibility for MAP credit

Under MAP A, free MAP Credit is distributed to the *firms* who are responsible for keeping this Credit equal to their Net Sales. The Credit could also be distributed in other ways, but giving the free Credit to firms and making them responsible for keeping their Net Sales and their MAP Credit equal has two major advantages:

(1)   Fluctuations in individual input prices are averaged out, which significantly reduces the problem of unmeasurable quality variations.

(2)   Most of the necessary information already exists at the firm level, since the firm is responsible for collecting payroll taxes, paying corporate income taxes, and maintaining records for audit. This significantly reduces the auditing problem.

Imposing the incentive at the firm level, however, means that the MAP disincentive is not always applied to the factor that is receiving the benefit of the higher price or wage. Instead, most of the disincentive falls directly on the firm, which *pays* the higher price or wage. In principle, this should not matter. It is an economic theorem that it is a matter of indifference who bears the statutory responsibility for the payment of a tax or who receives the subsidy. Since a MAP Credit is similar to a tax on raising price and a subsidy for lowering price, theoretically it should not matter who is directly responsible for its payment. In the long run, the net result will be the same. But it does present a potential short-run problem in that the firm that pays the higher factor income must also pay for the right to do this and the firm that lowers its factor income will also gain from the sale of MAP Credit.

Wages are the most important factor income in the United States, and this potential difficulty does not seem insurmountable in terms of wages. Firms are highly involved in setting wage rates and can take the MAP Credit price into account in their wage determinations. Where unions are intransigent in their demands for money wages, MAP could lead to strikes as firms tighten up on their money wage offers. Under MAP, however, workers would on the average receive the same *real* wages as before. Consequently, strikes—although possible—should not significantly increase. If the share of the total product of the economy going to wages remains the same, then total wages must increase at the same rate as the national average productivity increases. Thus, we would expect wage increases to average 2 percent per year. Firms might find it useful to grant larger wage increases even though these increases would cut into their own profits, unless the higher wages actually increased output by a greater amount than the increase in wages when this would be a wise investment. (The interest on money borrowed for this purpose would qualify the firm for additional free MAP Credit.)

Similarly, interest income does not seem likely to pose any potential difficulties. In MAP A, the interest the firm pays on new investment entitles it to additional free MAP Credit. As the firm's interest obligation changes because investments change, so too does its allowable Net Sales.

Some domestic products may present a problem because their prices are determined on the international market and are expected to rise. Firms producing such products will be required to buy MAP Credit continually to cover these rising prices. This will create an incentive to transfer ownership of the firm to noncovered or foreign sectors, so that the price can be raised without buying MAP Credit.

It is possible that we have underestimated the difficulties of implementing MAP on the firm level. If we have, MAP can be implemented on the individual level so that the incentive directly affects the individuals who receive the higher income (per *unit* of input). In such a MAP, any individual whose income increased above the normal income path would be required to buy MAP Credit, and individuals whose income fell below the norm would be able to sell MAP Credit. Adjustments could be made for inputs, as they are in MAP A. The disadvantages of this approach are administrative; determining the normal time path of income and measuring input adjustment on the individual level are both extremely difficult. On administrative grounds, therefore, we favor the firm-based MAP.

measurement of net sales

In measuring Net Sales, purchases from other firms that are not designed to be in-kind payments to factors (fringe benefits) will be subtracted from the firm's gross sales at the time of purchase. This way of measuring Net Sales corresponds to the "consumption" definition as distinguished from the "income" definition of "value added." The latter would subtract only the current depreciation allowance from gross sales, not the whole payment for capital goods purchased. We prefer the "consumption" approach, because it is administratively simpler and encourages investment. The "consumption" approach would allow Credit to increase relative to output of consumption goods during times of heavy investment. Thus, for technical reasons, this approach would permit a slight, temporary, upward movement of the price level during these periods.

Another issue in the measurement of Net Sales is determining which purchases to subtract from gross sales. For example, it would be possible to treat some factor prices, such as rent, as payments to other firms even though they are made to individuals. This would allow the firm to pass through increases (or decreases) in that factor price. Increasing "purchases from firms"—which is subtracted from gross sales in figuring Net Sales— reduces the measure of Net Sales, permitting prices to be raised to bring the figure up to the existing volume of MAP Credit. In general, this decision would be based on whether we want the increase in this factor price to be reflected in a rise in the price level (which would happen if the payment to the factor is treated as a purchase from other firms and subtracted from gross sales and therefore not counted in Net Sales) or whether we want it to be included in Net Sales (which would decrease the part of Net Sales going to the other factors). The relevant considerations are the relative cost of a movement in the price level compared with the cost of making the requisite reverse adjustments in money wages and profits.

The treatment of taxes can be viewed along these same lines. Taxes currently paid by the firm would be treated in the same way as payments to other firms; they would reduce the measured Net Sales of the firm and would already be reflected in current prices. Further changes in taxes could be treated in three different ways:

(1) Increased taxes could be treated as if they were payments to other firms. These payments would increase gross sales relative to real output without affecting Net Sales. Thus, the tax would take the form of an increase in the price level.

(2) The individual firm could be required to buy MAP Credit equal to the increase in taxes, reducing the remaining MAP Credit and Net Sales to the public to the point that makes them equal to the decrease in the amount of goods available to the public. This would neutralize the effect of the tax on the price level and lower overall factor incomes. The initial impact of the tax, however, would be to lower factor payments in firms that are statutorily responsible for the tax.

(3) The government could be required to buy MAP Credit equal to the increased tax revenue received. This would also neutralize the effect of the tax on the price level.

In all three cases, unless the tax is universal and neutral, the burden of the tax would shift among firms and employees. Any changes in taxes under a MAP program should specify precisely which of these three methods or what combination of them is to be followed.

Other problems in determining Net Sales include whether to use a present value or a cash flow approach in the treatment of deferred payments to factors and how to treat the appreciation of assets held by firms. However, these are technicalities, and arguments for and against various approaches to these questions have already been discussed at great length in connection with the income tax.

adjustments for inputs

MAP A provides for adjustments to be made in MAP Credit allowances— changes in labor inputs and in capital inputs. A number of alternative approaches are possible in both cases.

adjustments for labor inputs

MAP A utilizes the theoretically most complete method of allowing for changes in labor inputs: each worker carries his or her last wage rate from job to job, so that the current employer obtains the free MAP Credit allowance. This ensures that firms cannot manipulate their Net Sales by changing the skill mix or composition of their work force. An alternative approach would be to assign present wage rates to job *classifications,* rather than to individual workers. Thus, a new worker would adopt the wage rate at his or her new job classification. This approach would also involve administrative problems and would be subject to "wage drift" when job classifications are inflated. The choice between these two approaches must be based on specific institutional knowledge.

If problems of changing skill mix are not considered to be significant, a number of shortcuts are possible, such as the use of full-time employee or employee hours weighted by the average wage in the economy or by the average wage in that particular firm. This approach could be expected to increase the relative demand for below-average wage employees and to decrease the relative demand for above-average wage employees. Initially, these shortcuts would cause anomalies as high-wage firms hire additional low-wage employees, thereby lowering their measured Net Sales which would permit them to raise their prices without buying MAP Credit. Eventually, this would cause wages to move toward the mean and a new relative-wage equilibrium. If all sectors in the economy are not covered, using the average-wage measure will encourage the movement of high-wage individuals to noncovered sectors.

Numerous alternative methods could be employed to adjust for changes in the labor input, but none seem to offer the advantages of full-wage adjustment. However, we remain open-minded, because fairly significant administrative difficulties can arise if the full-wage adjustment is used. These problems include the need to calculate fringe benefits at the individual level, which will be especially difficult in handling group benefits. Similarly, hours will have to be measured at the individual level. This is not difficult to do for wage employees, but salaried employees will need to be assigned a "normal" number of hours.

Other problems include how to treat first-job workers, employees who transfer from a noncovered sector, retired workers who have shifted to less strenuous jobs, and employees who work overtime.

Possible ways to treat new workers include:

(1) Assigning all new employees a set wage (say, a minimum wage).

(2) Using the worker's initial wage as his or her base wage.

If the second approach is followed, the allowable MAP Credit would have to be restricted to the lower of the actual wage or the initial wage. This "minimum" requirement would prevent collusion between firms and workers in that a firm could not pay a worker a high initial wage to qualify for more MAP Credit and then lower the wage later. A similar downward "minimum" requirement would avoid the "retired individual" problem that would occur if a firm hires a previously highly paid retiree to perform a low paying job for the sake of acquiring MAP Credit.

A problem arises in the opposite direction when individuals increase their productivity by developing specialized skills, by self training, or merely by putting forth increased effort on the job. For example, if a husband worked as a secretary to put his wife through school and later became a lawyer, should the law firm hiring him be granted additional MAP Credit equal to the change in his wage? Under MAP A, the answer is no, but various adjustments could be made to encourage the acquisition of skills. One possibility is to provide educational institutions with MAP Credit which they can allocate to individuals who obtain degrees. Thus, an individual who completes high school could be allocated a specified base MAP Credit to be applied to his or her first job. Individuals who attend college or technical school could receive a specified increase per school year in their base MAP Credit. Many other adjustments could be made, but we will leave it to our more imaginative readers to devise them.

The adjustments that are made will not be perfect, and although they are significant, their importance can be overestimated. Each firm would have considerable flexibility in dealing with individual problems. MAP would control only the average net sales per unit of input. The allowable 2 percent increase in MAP Credit each year is designed to cover "impossible cases," and the firm can allocate it in various ways in solving problems. The law of large numbers hides innumerable sins.

adjustments for capital inputs

Measuring the flow services of capital is a difficult issue, and no practical measure will be perfect. MAP A adjusted for capital services by multiplying the change in stocks, bonds, and loans of a firm by the interest rate.

We chose this "flow of financial capital services" method because it seems relatively simple to discuss and to employ. However, its implementation does present some problems, such as deciding the relevant allowable interest rate and monitoring the flows. MAP is not tied to this approach to measuring the capital services input. Several other approaches can be considered.

One alternative would be to allow a pass-through of interest and dividends into Net Sales as if they were payments to others firms, as long as the interest or dividend rate does not exceed the initial interest rate paid by that firm. If the interest rate increases, the increase would still be treated in the same way as an increase in the rate of pay to other factors: it would not qualify the firm for additional free MAP Credit. Because both the interest rate and the dividend rate are expected to decline as inflation decreases, this approach may turn into a full pass-through approach, which would be even simpler and would not pose any administrative difficulties. All the interest payments could then be treated as payments to other firms.

Still another approach would be to allow free MAP Credit for the full amount of new investment in the year that the new investment is made (instead of adjusting only for the interest on the investment) and thereafter not to allow any further adjustments. This would subsidize net investment and tax net disinvestment, thereby providing what some economists call a strong "pro-investment bias." (For firms that maintain a constant rate of investment, this bias disappears.)

Because all these measures are calculated in terms of *adjustments* in MAP Credit to changes in Net Sales, the existing flow of total Net Sales will be "grandfathered" into the firm. Thus, if a firm buys back all its stock and redeems all its bonds, it may have a remaining capital stock of MAP Credit.

Canceling this possible source of a continuing income to a firm that has closed down (as long as the rental price of MAP Credit is positive) may be considered justifiable on equity grounds.

Initially, we had considered the alternative of not measuring the capital inputs and measuring only *Net Sales per employee.* Such an approach would be the easiest method to administer and would be adequate as long as the firm's capital–labor ratio did not change over time. But it is unreasonable to expect this. Apart from external reasons for such changes, firms would have an incentive to reduce their capital–labor ratios. This would enable them to reduce their factor payments while maintaining their Net Sales, or to increase their Net Sales without increasing their factor payments. Both of these changes (or any combination of them) would be inflationary. This also discriminates against investment in physical capital, just as using the number of employees in the measurement of the labor input discriminates against investment in human capital. This approach would also pose another aspect of the same problem: firms with high capital–labor ratios could enter industries with low capital–labor ratios. Some method of offsetting these possibilities would be needed if this measure were used.

The MAP proposal is not tied to any one particular measure of capital input. At present, we favor one of the flow-value measures of capital service input, but as more study is given to the administrative and theoretical problems posed by the various measures, another may emerge as superior.

integrating MAP into the pricing policies of firms

Under MAP A, the firm would be required to equalize its Net Sales to its MAP Credit every year. However, because many firms set their prices annually and do not know what their Net Sales will be until well into the following year, this may be too short a time period for firms fully to incorporate MAP into their pricing policies. Extending the time period in which the firm must meet the MAP requirements is one way to avoid this potential problem. Thus, a firm that had an especially good year, instead of buying the necessary MAP Credit, could decide to lower its prices during the next year—and thereby lower its average Net Sales for the two-year period.

An alternative approach to the yearly application of the Net Sales rule would be to use a three-year moving average, which would even out a firm's good and bad years. To avoid the problem of last-minute trading in MAP Credit, the ending period for firms could overlap. Which of these methods should be used can only be decided by experts who have specific institutional knowledge.

enforcement and auditing

MAP is a law. It will succeed only to the degree that a law can be enforced. Enforcement in turn, depends on the public's belief in the fairness and the necessity of the law. For this reason, careful auditing to discourage cheating will be necessary if MAP is to be implemented successfully.

The enforcement of MAP could either be integrated into the tax courts or left to the Justice Department. Clear cases of fraud would naturally be left to the Justice Department.

Penalties would be similar to the penalties for tax evasion. Since most of the necessary information will already have been collected by the Internal Revenue Service for tax purposes, auditing could most easily be integrated into the IRS tax audits.

conclusions

There are many other ways of adjusting the free MAP Credit for capital input. MAP could assume one of many alternative structures. Our own progression from one alternative method to another demonstrates the flexibility of the concept. How careful we need be in choosing among the different possible structures depends on the expected normal price of MAP Credit. If the expected price is zero or close to zero, little notice need be taken of complications. If, however, MAP Credit continues to sell for a high price for a long time, fine adjustments can be made while the program is in operation, just as adjustments are made to close tax loopholes.

8

the problems of starting up MAP

The introduction of MAP poses three problems:

(1) Determining the initial allocation of MAP Credit.
(2) Deciding how quickly to implement MAP.
(3) Determining how to integrate MAP initially into the planning and pricing policies of firms.

MAP A allocates initial MAP Credit according to Net Sales per unit of input in the year preceding the imposition of MAP. This may be insufficient for two reasons. First, some firms may have had a poor profit year and others may have had an excellent profit year. Second, some workers may have just received wage increases and others may be due for wage increases in the near future. Both of these issues constitute initial inequities in the MAP program that will require adjustments to the initial allocation of free Credit.

These adjustments can be achieved in two ways:

(1) *The administrative approach.* Set up boards to adjust the initial allocations of MAP Credit to allow for exceptionally high or low profits in the preceding year and to revise the wage contracts, setting the initial wage rates where they would have been if all wage contracts had been negotiated simultaneously.
(2) *The formula approach.* Instead of a board, a formula is used to average the Net Sales for several previous years. The average could give more weight to the more recent years and each year's Net Sales could be adjusted by the national average rate of inflation up to the time of the introduction of MAP. The same formula could be suggested as a reasonable basis for the renegotiation of wage contracts in light of the change in inflation expectations that would occur with the introduction of MAP.

Such adjustments are not easy to implement. The administrative approach requires difficult discretionary decisions to be made that are bound to come under political scrutiny; the formula approach will inevitably result in some examples of unfairness. We do not underestimate the complexities of these problems. However, they are decisions that must be made in any incomes policy. Under MAP, they will be easier to make than under any other

59

form of incomes policy, because MAP allows for relative price and wage flexibility. A faulty initial allocation of MAP Credit would not lead to shortages. but would merely require the firm to buy or sell MAP Credit as it adjusts its Net Sales. The importance of the initial distribution of Credit depends on how high the price of MAP Credit is expected to be. If it is high, the initial distribution will be important and a decision one way or another will involve significant wealth transfers. If the price of MAP Credit is low, the initial distribution will be relatively unimportant. As long as the accompanying macro policy does not generate excess demand, mainstream economic theory predicts that the price of MAP Credit will be close to zero as soon as the expectations of continuing inflation are dissipated by MAP's elimination of actual inflation. MAP should therefore present no serious problem.

Of the two methods, we feel that the formula approach is preferable because it avoids the difficult administrative questions on a case-by-case basis. Finding the perfect formula will be difficult, but time spent in establishing the formula will preclude innumerable administrative decisions later. If it takes a long time to agree on the formula and this delays the introduction of MAP, some method of avoiding pre-MAP price increases will need to be found. The best method would probably be to base initial free MAP Credit on the Net Sales of some earlier period.

a gradual MAP

MAP A immediately adjusted the inflation guideline down to zero. The desirability of doing this will depend on the ability of individuals to adjust pre-existing contracts made in the legitimate expectation that inflation would continue. Stopping inflation so suddenly violates expectational equity just as the initial surge in inflation violates expectations of a constant price level. How serious are the inequities that would be caused by a sudden halt to inflation is unclear. Many contracts, including almost all home mortgages and many business bonds, already contain a downward escape clause as a hedge against decreases in inflation. Other contracts might be renegotiated with some government compensation if important injustices remain. However, renegotiation of existing contracts is difficult and legally questionable.

As an alternative to its immediate cessation, the inflation could be reduced gradually at, say, a rate of 2 percent per year. Thus, if the pre-MAP inflation rate were 10 percent, it could be reduced to zero over a five-year period. This could be accomplished by increasing the initial allocation of MAP Credit by the estimated rate of inflation at the beginning of the MAP era. In this example, MAP A Credit would be increased by 8 percent in the first year and then reduced by two percentage points each year in the four following years. Shorter or longer periods of gradual disinflation could also be chosen. The length of time is not critical to MAP.

MAP is designed to keep trading in MAP Credit to a minimum by employing normal costs and profits as a guideline. Of course, there will be occasional deviations, but only minor trading should be required on the average. Even though the need for actual trading will be minimized, it is important that MAP not function as a retroactive tax but that it be integrated into the planning and pricing decisions of the firms. This will be difficult in the initial stages of the MAP program, because the price of MAP Credit will be unknown and the intricacies of the market will not be fully worked out.

To meet this problem, the government could follow one of two methods. It could set an initial price on MAP Credit for a specific time period and guarantee to buy and sell MAP Credit to fill demand at this price. In this introductory period, MAP would work just like a tax-based incomes policy. The deficit or surplus of MAP Credit from these transactions would indicate if the price were too low or too high, and the price would be adjusted from time to time to keep the balance as close to zero as possible.

Although this method is operable, it does interfere with MAP's ability to set the rate of inflation in the covered sector. Therefore, we favor a transition, as soon as it appears possible, to the alternative method of setting the quantity instead of the price of MAP Credit. The transitional period would give firms ample time to adjust their wage rates, investments, and prices in accord with the MAP guideline, so that they would be free not to buy or sell MAP Credit. Meanwhile, the free trading of MAP Credit at market set prices would permit firms to acquire a "feel for the market" before actually being *required* to buy or sell MAP Credit.

None of the solutions we have discussed here is ideal; each represents an administrative complication in the implementation of MAP A. In judging the importance of these complications, however, it is important to keep in mind that these are introductory problems, not ongoing problems, and that according to standard theory the price of MAP Credit is expected to be very low, if not zero, as soon as it is obvious that the inflation has really been stopped. Viewing MAP as an investment in future price stability will keep these problems in proper perspective.

coordination with macro policy

Because the price of MAP Credit is so central to the successful introduction of the program, it is essential that aggregate spending in the economy be coordinated with the introduction of MAP so that the growth in nominal aggregate spending is kept in proportion with the real growth of the economy.

A high initial MAP Credit price is an indication that expectations of above-guideline inflation are strong. If this continues after enough time has elapsed for most people to realize that the inflation has stopped (MAP A) or that it has been reduced to the chosen positive inflation guideline (8 percent in our example), the high price of MAP Credit will indicate that there is too much total spending in the economy as a whole and will be accompanied by shortages and the growth of black markets throughout the economy. This is the signal MAP provides to tell the authorities to reduce the rate of increase in total spending.

Moreover, it should be made clear that MAP will not achieve the exact planned rate of inflation (zero or otherwise) in any one year, but only on the average over a number of years. This is because although MAP sets total expenditures (Net Sales) by clear rules, there is some variability in total real output from changes in harvests and in productivity, from social and natural disturbances, and from fluctuations in imports, as well as some avoidance and evasion. The price level will also be subject to some variation if all economic sectors are not covered by MAP. The general price level can fluctuate to reflect changes in the non-covered sectors. Since, by design, the noncovered sectors are highly competitive, these price level changes will be temporary. They may affect the price level in a given year, but they should not affect the average price level over an extended period of time.

why fighting inflation will be easier than expected

Despite the difficulties inherent in fighting inflation, there are indications that it will be easier to stop or slow the inflation than expected. First, inflation is self-perpetuating: it is built on expectations. As inflation stops and people begin to believe that whatever stopped it will continue to work, the expectations of inflation themselves will decline. As expectations of inflation decrease, so too will the price of MAP Credit.

This argument assumes that people do not suffer from money illusion—from a belief that they are actually better off when the price level rises and their incomes rise in the same proportion. We do not believe in money illusion. In fact, given the publicity inflation has received, it is more likely that people currently suffer from the reverse illusion. They seem to believe that inflation hurts them more than it actually does. If this is the case, stopping inflation will make people feel better off even if they receive no more real income.

Second, inflation is actually a combination of two types of price increases: increases in the prices of domestic products and increases in the domestic prices of imports. The prices of imports depend on the exchange rate. As the inflation rose, there was a fall in the relative value of the dollar in foreign currency more than in proportion to the domestic price inflation. This occurred, in part, because individuals expected the inflation to continue. Thus, the dollar became less attractive to hold compared with the currency of countries with less inflation. This further aggravated the decline in the value of the dollar as the dollar came to be used less and less as a reserve currency. The decline in the dollar caused import prices to rise, thereby increasing inflation rates in the United States. If inflation subsides, this process will be reversed: the exchange rate will rise and the import prices will fall. This would temporarily lower the rate of inflation.

Third, high nominal interest rates are caused to a significant degree by inflation. These high interest rates, which are primarily a reflection of the expectations of inflation, push prices up even further as interest cost is built into prices. One example of this phenomenon is the current cash cost of home ownership, which is so high largely due to high interest rates. Decreasing inflation will lower interest rates, which will lower prices and inflation even further.

These are temporary phenomena that to some degree only affect illusions and rigidities in the system. They do not cause and they do not stop inflation. They merely accentuate upward or downward tendencies that already exist within the system—increasing or decreasing the degree of inflation.

the development of the MAP credit market

Another problem that the introduction of MAP will pose is the development of an institutional framework within which MAP Credit can be bought and sold. Such questions may arise as: How will trades be guaranteed? What type of sales will be permitted? Who will be allowed to trade? Can private individuals speculate in the market?

Some difficulties may be encountered in setting up a market for a completely new commodity like MAP Credit, but we do not see why it would be any more difficult to trade than Treasury bills or IBM shares on the stock exchange. Indeed, we are greatly encouraged by the development of the options market, which has spread to five exchanges in a little over five years and has reached a trading volume of 79 percent the size of the volume traded on the New York Stock Exchange.

If MAP Credit seems unusual, the options market must seem unbelievable. An option is an entitlement to buy a stock at a specified price at a certain time in the future. An entitlement trades on the market at a fluctuating price dictated by the expected price of the share and the striking price of the option (the stock price at which the option becomes operative). The higher the expected price of the share relative to the striking price, the higher the option price.

The development of the options market is not a concern of this book. However, the fact that such a market can independently spring to life should serve to ease the skepticism some MAP critics have expressed about the possibility of establishing a market for MAP Credit within a short period of time.

MAP and functional finance

deficits do not cause inflation

One of the reasons the current inflation is so pernicious is that it has thrown economic theory back to a neoclassical economic world in which the market can do no wrong. Although the authors are both great believers in the market and recognize that it has many virtues, in our view it is not infallible and works only with proper guidance. The economy needs a steering wheel.

If our forefathers had been as omniscient as rational expectationalists[1] would have us believe, they would have designed the system to operate on automatic control, so that it could optimally adjust to any economic circumstance. We do not doubt the logic of this viewpoint; we merely doubt the omniscience of our forefathers.

One of the most important economic lessons we thought had been learned over the last 30 years is that deficits do not cause inflation, but it seems to be necessary for this to be learned all over again. If the government decides to finance a new project by selling bonds, we say that it incurs a *deficit* and that this is inflationary. But if a firm does the same thing and enters the transaction on the capital account (not on the current account of the firm's budget), we call it an *investment* instead of a deficit, and the act is not considered inflationary.

Governments could also set up capital accounts, but a change in labeling solves no problems. It does not turn a bad decision into a good decision. The sensible criterion for government expenditure is whether or not the project is worthwhile from a social point of view, just as the sensible criterion for a firm's expenditure is whether or not the project is worthwhile from the firm's point of view. If a project is not worthwhile, it should not be undertaken—inflation or no inflation.

It is true that sound private investment increases productive capacity and lowers costs and prices in the future. But the same is also true of sound government investment. Products would be far more costly were it not for the transportation systems built by government. Similarly, without adequate legal systems or police protection, firms would find it difficult to carry out even

---

[1]See Colander (1979d).

64

everyday business transactions. Necessary government investment lowers future costs and prices in exactly the same way that necessary business investment does. Of course, unnecessary or wasteful investment—whether governmental or private—does not.

Nevertheless, there is a sound element hidden in the proposition that government budget deficits are inflationary. This can be brought into the light by opening up a budget to its three constituents: spending, taxing, and borrowing. This would indicate how and when these factors contribute to inflation.

The essential element is simply that whenever anyone increases his or her spending he or she increases total demand. If there is already more than sufficient total demand, increased spending will aggravate the excess demand and make the inflation more severe. However, if someone *reduces* spending, this produces the opposite effect. If the government increases its spending and simultaneously raises taxes by the same amount, the tax increase will induce taxpayers to reduce *their* spending—but by a *lesser amount* than the tax increase. Thus, there will still be a *net increase* in total spending and an intensification of any current demand inflation. Increasing taxation by a *greater amount* than the additional government spending is required to prevent this.

An exactly parallel argument applies if, instead of taxing, the government *borrows* the money, thereby running a deficit. In such cases, government borrowing will also reduce spending by lenders, but this reduction will probably be even less than the reduction in spending that results from increasing taxes. Thus *borrowing and spending* a certain amount *adds more* to total spending than *taxing and spending* the same amount does.

But all this is just as true of the private business borrowing and spending that we call investment. In both cases, the sensible criterion for judging the investment is the same—namely, whether the benefit is more than or less than the damage.

Clearly, an investment cannot be condemned just because—like a government deficit—it will increase total spending and will worsen the inflation if an excess demand inflation already exists. According to such logic, *all* investment, public and private—indeed all spending by anyone on anything—should be condemned.

The germ of truth hidden in the objection to deficits is that if there already is too much total spending, then *all* spending should be not condemned but *discouraged.* Every spending—including every investment—inflicts a social damage in that it aggravates the demand inflation.

The way to stop an excess demand inflation is to reduce total spending until demand is no longer excessive. But there is no reason to concentrate on reducing government investment or even on investment in general. *All* spending should be equally discouraged. Less urgent spendings would yield to more urgent spendings, so that only the least urgent of all spendings would be eliminated. The discouragement of spending in general to eliminate excess demand is the proper function of the Federal Reserve System. By restricting the money supply and raising the interest rate charged to everyone, the FED provides equal discouragement to all spenders, public and private, borrowers and lenders, investors and consumers—and it achieves the appropriate unequal responses. This eliminates any need for those who make investment decisions to take any further account of effects on total spending in the economy.

Whether or not total spending should be increased or decreased is another question that depends on the degree to which the capacity of the economy is utilized. When there is unused capacity, increased total spending will lead to growth; when there is not, increased total spending will lead to excess demand inflation. This is true whether the money is raised by taxing, by borrowing, or by using idle money, or whether the money is raised and spent by the government or by private business.

There is still much debate about the limits to growth or to increased output that are imposed by capacity constraints, by the mechanics of the process, or by the amount of control that the FED actually has (via the money supply) over total spending. For our purposes, it is sufficient to point out that if there is a connection between the deficit and inflation, it is through the effects *on total spending* of all the items that make up the deficit—the spending, the taxing, and the borrowing. There is no *direct* pipeline from the deficit to inflation.

It may seem strange that except for the reference to monetary and fiscal policy, this argument has been stated entirely in terms of "spending." "Money" has not been mentioned as a possible cause of demand inflation, even though too much money can be created by the monetary authorities. A middle-of-the-road expression would be that demand inflation is caused by "too much money chasing too few goods."

We find this formulation much more satisfactory, because it refers to the *activity* of money chasing goods, which is what we mean by *spending.* This is indeed what must really be meant by those who speak of *money,* or the quantity of money, as the fundamental cause of inflation. They certainly cannot mean that secretly printing money and locking it up in vaults would be inflationary. It is the *activity* of spending (which itself is sometimes due to expectations of spending) that really matters. The quantity of money (and of money substitutes) is significant only when it is actually being spent or when its availability makes it easier for someone to spend other money. This purely verbal difference is all that separates some "monetarists" from some "anti-monetarists." No harm is done by saying "money" or "money supply," if what is meant is the influence on *money spending.* Unfortunately, the terms "monetarist" and "anti-monetarist" often distinguish the holders of far more serious differences in opinion as to how the economy works.

MAP and employment

We have been deliberately vague about whether there is excess capacity in the economic system, both because we differ slightly in our estimates of how much slack there is in the economy and because the present state of macro theory on the matter is unsettled. We can differ on this point and still agree on the basic principles of MAP, because MAP is an anti-inflation program that can be integrated with any macro theory. The theoretical difference pertains to the effect MAP can have on total employment.

Whichever position one takes on this question, it should be clear that MAP will be unsuccessful unless it is integrated with the appropriate macro policy. This is why we placed the administration of the program with the FED. In the face of too much aggregate demand, MAP will merely become a form of price control. One important and interesting difference is that price controls would create shortages in some markets but not in others, whereas MAP would distribute these shortages equally among all sectors of the economy. Nonetheless, if total spending is too high, there will be shortages. The question is when is total spending too high?

Until MAP is imposed, this will remain a metaphysical question, because no measure of the intensity of total demand is available. This means that policy makers are now operating in the dark, much like a boiler man stoking a fire with no pressure gauge. Problems are inevitable.

As generally happens when empirical testing is difficult, if not impossible, metaphysical disagreements develop. Here, these take the form of a dispute as to whether the economy needs heating or cooling. Theories have been expounded suggesting the existence of a natural rate of unemployment that is coincidental with the actual rate of unemployment, regardless of its fluctuations. If such theories are true, no total spending increase can stimulate the economy. Others have argued that a 2-percent unemployment rate is sufficient to accommodate all the "frictional," "search," and "wait" unemployment required by a normal economy and that any greater unemployment rate cries out for government intervention. As of this writing, these debates are still proceeding.

Various alternative pressure gauges have been used. Unfortunately, in an inflationary economy the natural measure—the interest rate—is singularly inappropriate. What we want to measure is the *real* interest rate, but what we can measure is only the *nominal* interest rate, which includes unmeasurable expectations of future inflation. The inevitable result is confusion. An 8-percent interest rate may be high or low, depending on inflationary expectations. Both positions have been argued vigorously. An alternative measure is the unemployment rate, but unanswerable questions about what constitutes involuntary versus voluntary employment permits such leeway in interpretation that, despite all attempts, no agreement has been reached regarding the meaning of unemployment for an aggregate spending policy.

A significant advantage of MAP is that it adds another measure—the price of MAP Credit—as a gauge of the inflationary pressure in the economy. Changes in conditions of either aggregate supply or demand will be reflected in the price of MAP Credit, thereby providing policy makers with an additional guide to the appropriate aggregate spending policy.

This is, of course, the informational function of any price. However, instead of measuring the individual's desire for a good, the price of MAP

Credit measures the upward pressure on prices. This information, combined with information regarding the states of various markets, will provide new information about the economy which will permit all macro tools to operate more efficiently.

MAP and a monetary rule

Since it controls the price level, MAP will allow a monetary rule to be introduced. Previously, it has been impossible to implement a monetary rule due to its potential effect on unemployment if the price level were to rise drastically. MAP circumvents this problem. The monetary rule might set the growth of the money supply as a function of total inputs, the MAP Credit price, the price level in the noncovered sector, and the average productivity growth. Thus, given the zero or other inflation rate determined by MAP, there would never be too much or too little money in the economy.

This rule would give the money supply the needed elasticity to adjust to real changes in the economy, but at the same time it would provide the safeguards required to ensure that MAP does not become merely a form of controls.

Setting a rule for monetary policy does not eliminate the role of the Federal Reserve. A monetary rule requires an activist policy, because the short-term demand for money tends to fluctuate. Nor does a monetary policy eliminate the potential need for fiscal policy. Total spending in the economy can still be affected by a deficit financed by selling bonds. Under the monetary rule, this deficit could bring about an increase in the money supply only if additional money is needed to facilitate increased real activity in the economy. If a fiscal policy merely pushed up the price of MAP Credit and did not affect real output, it would not bring about an increase in real output, in total spending, or in the quantity of money.

If the strict monetarists are correct and there is no spare productive capacity in the economy, bond-financed expansionary fiscal policy will not increase real output or total spending but will merely crowd out private investments. If the fiscalists are correct and there is spare productive capacity in the economy, bond-financed fiscal policy *will* increase total real output and spending. It seems worthwhile to us to implement MAP, even if merely to put an end to this debate—one way or the other.

10

some technical issues

Obviously, this book is not written in the familiar economic style of Theorem → Proof → Theorem → Policy Conclusion. Instead, MAP employs a "realytic" methodology which emphasizes common-sense arguments rather than rigorous, analytic mathematical statements. This is a necessary approach. It would have been impossible to write about MAP in an analytic style, because MAP is so full of interesting and unanswered theoretical questions that the book would never have been finished and most of MAP's policy orientation would have been lost.

Nonetheless, we believe that numerous issues concerning MAP have analytic significance or need clarification. It will therefore be useful to incorporate MAP into present analytic models to achieve a better understanding of those models as well as of the workings of the actual economy and of MAP.

modeling MAP

You will find no rigorous mathematical model of MAP in this book. We rely instead on our intuitive practical model, which is a view of the way the economy works. This does not mean that we do not find models useful. It simply means that we do not believe a rigorous macro model of simultaneous inflation and unemployment exists. In fact, even a rigorous mathematical micro–macro model of the inflation process itself does not exist.

The problem is that inflation is a dynamic, general-equilibrium process, whereas most models are either partial-equilibrium or static models, or both. In a general-equilibrium model, aggregate supply and demand are interrelated and do not determine the price level or the level of output, as they do the price and the output in partial-equilibrium models. If either supply or demand shifts, so does the other. Aggregate supply and demand models which do not take this interrelationship into account cannot be used to deal with inflation. But the problem is even more severe. Inflation is a problem of price dynamics, and economics has only developed crude theories of price dynamics for partial-equilibrium models. No model of general-equilibrium price dynamics exists.

The lack of a meaningful model of inflation is generally recognized and attempts have been made to devise one. However, as soon as one begins to address the interesting questions, the mathematics becomes so complicated that analysts are forced to make simplifying assumptions that severely limit the relevance of the model.

These simplifying assumptions are useful as long as we keep in the back of our mind the real economy we are attempting to understand. However, when understanding the model becomes the end and not the instrument, the model has lost its purpose. This is what we fear has happened to much of the economic analysis of inflation.

If we had chosen to model MAP formally and mathematically, we would have used a general-equilibrium model in which MAP serves as an aid to the price-setters.[1] In such a model, MAP would coordinate the individual pricing decisions so that the price level remains constant. Thus, MAP can be viewed as the introduction of another commodity—MAP Credit, the right to raise Net Sales relative to factor inputs—and another equation in the determination of the total nominal income in the economy. The MAP Credit price is the price of this new commodity. The price has a zero value only if the system is in equilibrium; that is, if the system has been adjusted to current factor inputs and general productivity growth.[2]

It is a fundamental theorem of economics that if the economy is in equilibrium, excess demands sum to zero. However, given the institutions, a constant price level is *not* a necessary condition. If nominal excess demands sum to zero only at an unchanging price level, then the price of MAP Credit will equal zero only when there is no excess demand or supply. The appropriately weighted prices tending to fall will only then just equal those tending to rise. In fact, this is how we define equilibrium. Of course, an expectational element could keep the price of MAP Credit positive, but once those expectations are broken, the MAP Credit price would quickly decline to zero.

If there is a bias in the economy so that it tends to equilibrate at a rising price level, then the price of MAP Credit will be positive, thereby offsetting that bias and establishing a stable price level instead. The hypothesis that this condition persists when the system is in equilibrium in all other senses could be called the "dynamic cost push" hypothesis. The belief that MAP Credit will have a positive equilibrium price in the absence of expectational inflation, and without the shortages due to excess demand, is a useful way of distinguishing economists who believe that an element of "cost push" exists from pure "pull" theorists and pure expectationalists.

MAP, the Phillips curve, and unemployment

In discussing MAP, we have carefully avoided the trade-off between unemployment and inflation represented by the Phillips curve because we did not want to tie MAP to any one of the various theories underlying the trade-off. MAP will work regardless of the relationship between inflation and unem-

---

[1] Since TIP is an analogue to MAP, it should be modeled in the same way. Many analyses of TIP have been partial-equilibrium models, and have confused relative price changes with price level changes.

[2] Naturally, all the equivalent technicalities apply to the development of the appropriate indexes, as they do to the development of price indexes, but they do not change the substantive concept of the transposition of prices and quantities. The price increase of a product per unit of input is the commodity, and the quantity of inputs traded is the weight.

ployment. But an understanding of the nature of the Phillips curve becomes relevant to concluding whether MAP will allow an expansion in real output or whether it will merely stop the inflation.

If we assume that there is a natural rate of unemployment and that this rate is also the optimal rate of unemployment, then obviously any higher level of unemployment is suboptimal. This view seems to be implicit in many discussions about the natural rate of unemployment. According to this view, the economy can reach a lower level of unemployment only if the monetary authorities mislead the public. MAP would not allow any such increase in output, because MAP would force all changes to be real (not nominal) changes. On the natural rate hypothesis, an excess demand would never call forth any increase in supply. The price of MAP Credit would immediately push up the rental price of MAP Credit to 100 percent of its face value, and no one would want to buy or sell it because each dollar of MAP Credit would be exactly equivalent to one dollar. Similarly, any shortfall in demand would lower the MAP Credit price to *minus* 100 percent, and each unit of MAP Credit would be exactly equivalent to a debt of one dollar. Thus, on the natural rate of unemployment hypothesis, the MAP Credit price becomes a knife-edge.

We hold that the knife-edge view of MAP Credit price is implausible and that there will be various levels of demand and supply equality associated with various levels of the MAP Credit price. In other words, we suspect that no unique macro equilibrium exists. This view is implicit in Keynesian theory and formed the basis of Lerner's introduction of a range between a low full employment and high full employment.

We should make it clear that this view requires no assumption of money illusion. Individuals are fully aware of their real income and make their economic decisions on that basis. Total employment is limited by real aggregate demand, which is generally kept too low in inflationary situations. Higher aggregate demand can produce two possible effects: it can stimulate higher aggregate supply, or it can cause the price level to rise. Which it does depends on whether a method of controlling inflation exists. In the absence of money illusion, expectations of a rising price level will bring about an equilibrium at the expected rate of inflation, and expectations of an increasing rate of inflation will bring about an equilibrium at the expected rate of acceleration of inflation.

However, if a mechanism could prevent a one-time rise in price level from being built into expectations, the government would not be prevented from providing enough total spending to permit a higher level of activity without inflation. MAP provides such a mechanism. Whether higher levels of output are associated with a pressure for rising prices, which would be offset by the corresponding positive price of MAP Credit, is an interesting question we leave for more analytic economists to speculate about—and for experience with MAP to answer.

limits to the price of MAP credit

MAP Credit is a capital asset, but it can also be rented for a year. Its price as a capital asset can exceed its rental price. In general, the asset price will be equal to the discounted flow of income the Credit entitles the bearer to receive from raising the price of output per unit of input. If this did not increase an individual's income, MAP Credit would have no value. The possible price would be limited because the supply of Credit would flood the market before the rental price reached 100 percent of the face value—the value of the Net Sales it legitimizes.

economic adjustment under MAP

Another interesting question that arises is whether MAP will slow the adjustment process. To the degree that MAP hampers adjustment by discouraging firms from raising their prices, it also helps adjustment by encouraging other firms to lower their prices.

But even if MAP did affect the amount of short-run price fluctuations, how important this effect would be is unclear. Most of the items that would be included in MAP are priced more in accordance with their long-run rather than their short-run price. To labor, issues of job security and long-run promotion prospects are far more important than the short-run wage rate, and fixed capital is largely nonadjustable. Due to the nature of these factors, short-run prices do not fluctuate in most manufacturing sectors; instead, they are set by a stabilizing normal markup procedure. Although some shading (temporary discounts, etc.) occurs if the good is not selling properly, in general, the long-run price seems to be more important. MAP sets the allowable guideline for the firm at the long-run normal cost, so that on the average, it should closely parallel the firm's normal pricing policies.

When the price of MAP Credit is high, some additional rationing may be necessary in sectors where there are shortages, but more price cutting should occur in sectors that experience low demands. The net effect on the adjustment speed in the economy is unclear.

the role of profits under MAP

Under MAP, profits function as they do in our present economy—as a return to investment. MAP will not affect the expected value of these profits. It will only reduce their variance. This reduction in variance will reduce risk and therefore should increase the amount of investment in the economy.

Some concern has been expressed that because such a reduction in variance will reduce the relative profits of the more successful firms, it will be more difficult for these firms to finance additional investments from retained earnings. This is probably true, but we can see this effect of MAP as an advantage, rather than a disadvantage. There are two reasons for our view.

First, retained earnings are already subsidized, because personal income taxes are avoided when firms retain earnings instead of paying them out as dividends. This gives existing firms a comparative advantage in an expanding industry and discourages new entry. Potential competitors know that by the time they enter the market, the established firms will probably have expanded their capacity to the point that it will not be advantageous to consider entry. The important point is that the expected future price determines entry; this price has little to do with the current selling price. When there is little connection between the current price and expected future prices, high retained earnings operate as a barrier to entry, which in turn helps to maintain the high profits from the temporary monopoly. MAP will help to remove that barrier and thereby will help to promote competition.

Second, MAP removes a tendency toward inflation. The nominal wage standard is often set by the firm or industry with the highest wage increase. This increase, in turn, often occurs in the industry with the highest profits. By reducing the variance of profits, MAP reduces this institutional push so that the initial MAP Credit price will not need to be as high.

inefficiencies due to MAP

Allowing individuals to trade benefits those who voluntarily engage in the trade, but it guarantees that the system will be made more efficient only as long as that trading does not affect people who are not involved in the trade. For this reason, it is extremely important to consider external effects when judging the efficiency of any program.

When individuals set prices, they do not take into account the overall effect that their decisions will have on the price level. The effect on the price level is an externality. When there is inflation, by definition, more individuals are raising than are lowering their prices (weighted by quantity). MAP requires each individual to consider the effect of his or her economic decision on the price level, thereby internalizing the externality and eliminating this inflationary pressure.

In achieving this end, if we are relatively happy with the way the system is operating, we would also like to disturb the system as little as possible. MAP is designed to do precisely that. Naturally, the actual definitions used have not been perfectly correlated with their theoretically correct counterparts, so MAP may affect some real variables and incur some inefficiencies. It will do so, however, only if the MAP Credit price is a non-zero price. If it is positive, either there are underlying inflationary pressures in the economy that MAP is keeping under control or the economy is reaching a higher level of output than otherwise would be possible. In both cases, MAP is serving a real function. It is unreasonable to compare a non-zero price MAP world with a perfect MAPless world, because in that world MAP would have a zero price.

In the real world, there is an inflation problem and it must be met by a "real world" solution, such as tying the money supply to gold, wage and price controls, or sharp monetary restrictions. However, each of these solutions exhibits far more serious inefficiencies than MAP.

The concept of inflation as an externality is especially enlightening because it provides a method of reincorporating inflation into microeconomics. (Unemployment can also be treated in the same way.) Somehow, all the individual decisions must be coordinated. This is the function of the economic system. It is a difficult task that changes over time as the roles of various institutions in society evolve and are redefined. The market is a useful mechanism for coordinating activities, but we cannot assume that the coordination can always be achieved by the market without the development of new markets, rules, and collective actions.

It is in this view of the market that we differ from some monetarists who assume that because the old tools were good enough for our forefathers, they should be good enough for us. This attitude does not allow for adjustments so as to incorporate productivity advances in the workings of markets. In our view, a well-functioning society is an evolving society, and new problems must be handled as they arise from technological changes. MAP makes the market itself more efficient.

MAP credit price and productivity

The basis for MAP Credit is Net Sales per unit of input, which is how we define productivity. It has been argued that a positive MAP Credit price constitutes a tax on firms that must acquire MAP Credit to match increasing Net Sales and a subsidy to firms that can relinquish some of their MAP Credit to match decreasing Net Sales, and that this taxes efficiency or productivity and subsidizes inefficiency. In one sense this argument is correct; a positive MAP Credit price will have the effect of a tax on the nonquantifiable, relative improvements in inputs (intensity of effort, home-study improvement, etc.), and in this sense it will operate in a manner similar to an income tax. How important this effect is depends on the importance of the nonquantifiable, relatively improved inputs and on their relative elasticity of supply.

A positive MAP Credit price will encourage firms to switch from less quantifiable to more quantifiable inputs, for which they will receive more MAP Credit. This shift will produce a decrease in *measured* physical productivity. The decrease in measured productivity will merely reflect a flaw in the productivity measurement that is incorrectly assessing the productive contribution of the inputs. The real cost of this shift will only be the loss in output that results from the shift. This is not, however, the loss usually envisaged by the argument. It is in fact of a much smaller order of magnitude.

For *the economy as a whole,* the increase in productivity is provided for in the 2 percent automatic annual increase in MAP Credit and allowable total Net Sales, so that the increase in productivity takes the form of increased factor income rather than lowered output prices. A positive MAP Credit price is therefore not a tax on *overall* productivity.

For *an industry,* relative increases in productivity may raise or lower its Net Sales per unit of input, depending on the elasticity of the demand for its product. An increase in Net Sales would then indicate an increase in demand that was more than proportional to any reduction in price, which would constitute the appropriate incentive for the *expansion* of input. In the converse case, an increase in demand that is less than proportional to the reduction in price would result in decreased Net Sales and would call for the *contraction* of input. Both responses are appropriate. Increases and decreases in Net Sales do not indicate increases and decreases in *productivity,* but only increases and decreases in *scarcity*—both of which can result from an increase in productivity. The payments and receipts for MAP Credit constitute income equalization or compensatory insurance payments (like the payments made to farmers who suffer from too bountiful a crop or too poor a demand). High or low Net Sales encourages expansion in the case of scarcity and contraction in the case of oversupply. A positive MAP Credit price only serves as a tax on productivity gains that are *not passed on* in lower prices and as a subsidy to productivity gains that are *more than passed on* in lower prices. It is not a tax on productivity per se and lasts only until the size of the industry adjusts to the change.

For the *individual firm* that experiences an increase in productivity compared with other firms in the same industry, the demand (for the output of the firm) is highly elastic, so that there is an increase in profit and the increase in productivity is not passed on in lower prices. The profit is then reduced by the cost of the additional MAP Credit that the firm is required to buy. If the increase in the firm's productivity results from its adoption of a generally available new method before other firms do so, this is identical to the case of an industry and lasts only until the other firms increase their productivity. But if the increase in a firm's productivity is the result of special efforts or enterprise (which are nonquantifiable inputs), the payment for the additional MAP Credit does discriminate against efficiency. This is the result of the bias against nonquantifiable inputs discussed earlier and is the only case in which the argument that the MAP Credit price is a tax on productivity is correct.

Since MAP allows additional Credit for investments in productivity gains, such investments are not discouraged. (These investments include research, development, training, and even hiring managers to determine better ways to organize existing inputs.)

Under MAP, productivity will still be rewarded because competition will force out inefficient firms. The more efficient firms can expand their market share by underpricing the less efficient firms. There will be a stronger incentive toward such competition under MAP. In fact, a positive MAP Credit price turns out to be only a tax on monopolization.

MAP credit price operations and total output

A positive MAP Credit price might be viewed as a subsidy on hiring inputs and as a tax on the value of output. To the degree that the subsidy on the inputs equals the tax on the output, MAP will have no effect either on total output or total inputs. However, this will not always be the case.

Often the inputs are employed in one period and the outputs occur during a later period. The MAP subsidy would apply at the time the input is employed; the tax would become effective later when the output is sold. The firm's net gain or loss is the difference between the initial "subsidy" and the discounted value of the "tax." If the MAP Credit price is expected to remain constant, there will be no net subsidy or tax. If the MAP Credit price is expected to decline, this constitutes an expected subsidy on the postponement of output (that is, on investment) and creates an expectation of lower prices in the future. Conversely, an expected rise in the price of MAP Credit constitutes a tax on the postponement of output and creates an expectation of higher prices in the future. Such parallel movements of MAP Credit price and commodity prices as total Net Sales becomes stabilized by MAP could lead to minor price oscillations.

But here there is no free lunch. The MAP subsidy involves a slight upward movement in the current price level as resources are moved from the production of current output to investment for future output. This is similar to a tax on present consumption and a subsidy on future consumption. The converse is true of an expected rise in the price of MAP Credit.

If certain institutional constraints exist, MAP can influence total employment in another way. If the price of MAP Credit is positive and workers who differ in ability must be paid an identical wage, either due to union rules or minimum wage laws, some workers may be unemployed because their marginal product is less than the standardized wage. MAP would reduce the net cost to the firm of hiring an additional worker by providing an amount of MAP Credit for the individual greater than his or her productivity. Thus, MAP would make it worthwhile to expand employment. This subsidy would be paid for by a one-time upward movement in the price level as MAP Credit and Net Sales increase more than output, thereby reducing the real wage of all other individuals. Whether total real output increases or decreases will depend on the response of the other individuals to the rise in the price level.

MAP and the foreign sector

When the rate of domestic inflation exceeds the rate abroad, this tends to lower the relative value of the currency. At times, the interpretation of this relationship is reversed by economists who suggest that the decline in the relative price of a currency generates the inflation. It is true that since MAP allows import prices to pass through, the price level can increase as the relative value of our currency decreases. The higher price level brings about the necessary reduction in real income that must accompany the decline. But, by placing a lid on total domestic Net Sales, MAP stops the initial price rise from generating an internal inflation.

A similar argument holds for a rise in the domestic price of an imported good for any other reason. MAP permits the necessary price rise but prevents the domestic inflationary response. When a good is produced both at home and abroad, a rise in import prices causes the price of import-competing goods to rise also. To raise their prices, domestic firms would be required to buy Credit, which can come only from other domestic firms who lower their Net Sales. Thus, MAP operates both as a type of excess profits tax on firms experiencing windfall gains from external price fluctuations and as an adjustment subsidy to firms experiencing windfall losses.

If the economy has a fixed exchange rate which exceeds the equilibrium exchange rate, the government no longer has total control over the money supply or total spending because it must use its fiscal and monetary instruments to maintain external balance. Thus, the necessary integration of

MAP with functional finance will be difficult, if not impossible, to achieve. Total spending will have to be adjusted to the exchange rate, rather than the reverse. A flexible exchange rate dissolves this problem.

Since inflation will be stopped under MAP, we would expect the relative value of the dollar to improve significantly. As long as inflations continue abroad, the relative value of the dollar will continue to increase and it will become more and more attractive as a reserve currency for foreign central banks than it has ever been.

conclusion

These are, of course, only some of the technical issues that might be raised about MAP. And each issue we have introduced here raises other questions that we have left unanswered. We hope that other economists will explore these technical aspects further as they consider how MAP might fit in with their particular view of the economic process.

other novel proposals

Necessity is the mother of invention, and the failure of macroeconomics to cope with inflation has spawned a number of novel proposals. Some of these are practical policy proposals that have been considered by governments; others are merely conceptual sketches that seem to make sense to their creators but their practicality has not yet been examined. In this chapter, we will comment briefly on some of the proposals that have come to our attention.

Two well worked out policy proposals have a direct relation to MAP: tax-based incomes policies and indexation.

taxed-based incomes policies

The development of MAP has been greatly influenced by the discussions of the theoretical and practical aspects of tax-based incomes policies that have taken place over the last few years. The economics profession owes a large debt to its originators: M. Scott (1961), H. Wallich (1971), S. Weintraub (1971), L. Seidman (1976, 1978), A. Okun (1978), and the Hungarian Government (Portes, 1970). Lerner's interest in MAP originated from a discussion about TIP with Larry Seidman, and many practical decisions about the MAP proposal were based on such analyses of TIP as L. Dildine and E. Sunley's (1978) and R. Slitor's (1978).

MAP, in turn, has much to contribute to TIP. Theoretically, it is difficult to understand the workings of TIP without understanding MAP. This is because *inflation is a dynamic, general-equilibrium problem of the price level* and not a partial-equilibrium problem of relative prices. Many theoretical discussions of TIP have focused on partial-equilibrium models of what would happen to an individual firm's relative prices, as if the tax-based incomes policy were to be imposed only on one firm and as if TIP did not need to be integrated with aggregate policy. In our view, these models are irrelevant to TIP and are primarily displays of mathematical virtuosity.

The best way to view TIP theoretically is as a tax analogue to the equivalent market-based incomes policy. The TIP tax necessary to offset inflation is precisely the price of MAP Credit. It therefore follows that, like MAP, a TIP tax operates primarily through expectations. If an individual firm does not believe that other firms are going to raise their prices, there will be no need for it to raise its price. TIP and MAP will succeed in getting people to believe that inflation will be stopped by making them observe that the inflation has stopped. Because these inflationary expectations are so important, it is essential that TIP or MAP be coordinated with macro policy—something that its advocates have stressed but that its modelers have often forgotten.

Viewing TIP as an analogue to MAP also suggests several desirable characteristics of TIP:

(1) The guideline should be based on Net Sales per unit of input instead of on wages or profits or prices.
(2) TIP should include both a subsidy and a tax.
(3) The program should be self-financing.
(4) The TIP tax should be implemented as a separate excise tax and not as part of a corporate income tax or a payroll tax; the TIP subsidy should be treated similarly.
(5) TIP should be a permanent, not a temporary, program.
(6) TIP should provide an equal incentive proportional to all changes in Net Sales and not be instituted as an "either-or" or "hurdle" incentive.
(7) A TIP tax should be seen not as a penalty, but as an incentive.

A TIP with these characteristics would be very similar to MAP. If the MAP proposal could not be applied for some reason, we would support such a TIP. But we prefer MAP even to such a "perfected" TIP for three reasons:

(1) The correct disinflationary offset is never known, but markets can provide information about the required incentive. The market price of MAP Credit, which is the disinflationary incentive, will automatically find the required level to offset the inflationary pressures. This will allow the policy maker to establish a desired level of inflation; the MAP credit price will then gravitate to the required level. Under TIP, the policy maker must set the price of the incentive and allow the quantity of inflation to vary.
(2) The inflationary pressure to be offset by the MAP Credit is bound to vary over time, if only as a result of the operation of the anti-inflation policy. The MAP Credit price will continuously adjust to the changes. In theory, the TIP tax could also be raised and lowered to correspond to changing inflationary pressures, but this can only be done after the fact. Thus, the control of inflation is far less direct under TIP. Moreover, even if it could be achieved theoretically, the political realities suggest that varying taxes frequently is unfeasible.
(3) MAP is designed to keep politics and discretionary governmental action out of the program. This is why control of the implementation of MAP was placed with the FED. A TIP would be integrated into the tax system and therefore would be more subject to political pressures.

We recognize, however, that precisely because MAP takes the control away from the political process, it is likely to be politically more difficult to implement. *MAP would solve inflation,* but until the political powers actually *want* to stop inflation—rather than merely to *appear to* want to stop inflation—MAP will not be implemented. A TIP is more likely to be adopted.

indexation

Another policy that has received serious attention is indexation, which consists of setting all contracts in real, not nominal, terms. It should be made clear that indexation is not a solution to inflation. More precisely indexation is an aid to living with inflation. Advocates nevertheless claim that indexation would also help to fight inflation in three ways:

(1) Full indexation would avoid the expectational equity arguments against ending inflation too quickly. If all contracts are fully indexed, decreases in inflation will not hurt individuals because the contracts will be immediately adjusted.

(2) Indexation would shorten the lag time that it takes for a reduction in total spending to have its full effect.

(3) Indexation would stop the government's "inflation ripoff."

Although we agree with many of the arguments in favor of indexation, in our view, this policy proposal has substantial drawbacks as an instrument for fighting inflation.

First and most important is the technical issue of timing. Contracts are agreements that are made before other prices are known. When a price is set, it is based on the expectations of what other prices will be. Some of these expectations will be wrong, and therefore the prices set will be incompatible with one another. Setting contracts in terms of money allows some flexibility in the adjustment of the price level if some of the initial decisions are inconsistent. If the majority of errors are on the up side, the price level rises. If the majority of errors are on the down side, the price level declines. But if the system is fully indexed, no flexibility is possible. And if the initial prices are inconsistent, some contracts are unfulfillable. Indexation would work only if the market always anticipated the correct set of equilibrium prices instead of arriving at it by trial and error. But, if this were possible, there would be little need for the market, whose primary function is to provide a method of adjusting to equilibrium.

In principle, it would be possible to employ a type of contingent indexation that would allow relative price flexibility contingent on certain events. However, the enormous administrative costs of implementing such a procedure would preclude its consideration as a practical alternative.

The second problem posed by indexation is closely related to the first. If the contracts are indexed, which index should be used? Most advocates of indexing suggest that it would be preferable to tie contracts to the Consumer Price Index (CPI).

This index would present serious problems. If all contracts are tied to the CPI and the price of imports suddenly rises due to a monopolization of those imports, the CPI would rise. This would force all wages to rise and, in turn, all product prices to rise, thereby raising the CPI. Thus, such a system would explode. The fundamental problem is that there would be less to go around for everyone. A drop in real income is inevitable, but fixing all contracts in real terms decrees that real income will not decline. In this particular example, the difficulty can be removed by using a domestic output price index. But a reduction in domestic output would produce a similar crisis.

The claim that indexation would stop the government "ripoff" associated with inflation as a hidden tax that needs no legislation, is a naive one. It depends on more consumer irrationality than we are willing to assume. Somehow the general population is not supposed to realize that inflation, insofar as it provides resources for the government, must hurt them at least as much as when the government raises the same resources by taxation. In our view, consumers are more intelligent and realize the effects of a substantial inflation. In fact, they are probably more likely to fail to support a government that exploits inflation as a "hidden tax" to raise money than a government that raises their taxes by an equivalent amount.

In our view, government is as much a victim of inflation as the rest of us (and the rest of us are as culpable of perpetrating inflation as the government). Asking the government to stop increasing the volume of total spending and the quantity of money in the face of continuing inflation is as fruitless as asking business to stop increasing prices in the face of increasing costs or asking labor to stop demanding money wage increases in the face of increasing prices. The question for all of us is how do we escape from this vicious circle.

Despite these arguments, as we stated earlier, we are sympathetic to indexation. In fact, Lerner has long been an advocate of indexation, but only to ameliorate the inequities that stem from impending inflation. The questions that need to be answered are how to achieve this and which index to employ. MAP ties the purchasing power of money to a composite price of factor inputs, not product outputs. This retains the flexibility that will be required when real changes occur. One of the beauties of MAP is that it can be said to provide indexation and, at the same time, to preserve the function of money.

other market proposals

In addition to these two major policy proposals, a number of other sketchy concepts bear some resemblance to MAP. They include two plans for controlling inflation, a "free market in money" proposal, and direct relativity bargaining. Although they vary in theoretical approach, several of these are based on the same line of reasoning as MAP.

Two market proposals by J. V. Howard (1976) and Christian von Weitzäcker (1976) are similar to MAP in that they employ permits and the market to control inflation. However, rather than approaching the issue as an extension of incomes policies, their proposals incorporate two quite different perspectives.

Howard's proposal

Howard's proposal is based on a value-added measure—as is MAP. It would issue firms "income certificates" equal to a fixed amount of value-added for each individual hired and would force firms to trade certificates until they obtained sufficient certificates to cover their value-added.

Despite these similarities, however, Howard's proposal exhibits important differences from MAP, which follow from his underlying approach. It is designed to control the "flow of spending" and thereby the price level. MAP is designed to control the price level and thereby the flow of spending per unit of input. Thus, Howard's proposal is an extension of a monetarist model, whereas MAP is an extension of an incomes-policy model.

This difference is significant because of the way in which Howard's proposal allocates certificate spending. Howard's plan allocates income certificates to firms on the basis of the number of employees they hire. This would grant the firm the right to an income flow of more than the employee's wage. The MAP Credit price applies pressure on firms with rising total factor incomes. Howard's proposal concentrates the pressure on capital-intensive firms. It follows that if the price of certificates is positive, capital-intensive firms would be severely discriminated against and would need to buy additional certificates. In long-run equilibrium, this would lower the return on investment and thereby hamper capital formation.

As long as the required pressure is not strong, this difference will not be significant; however, if a strong pressure is necessary, significant distortions will be introduced in Howard's proposal and the system will break down.

For example, if labor-intensive firms with spare certificates from decreased output and employment decide that instead of selling them, they will use these certificates to raise their factor payments, the flow of money income will not be altered, but the amount of available real income will be reduced. The capital-intensive sector will then have the option of lowering its price or paying whatever certificate price is demanded by the labor-intensive sector. The problem will be solved if competition forces the factor price down. But if competition forces the factor price to decrease immediately, the proposal is not needed. Howard's proposal forces significant trading in certificates. MAP attempts to minimize the necessary trading in MAP Credit.

We should point out that Howard's plan was only a sketch and not a completed proposal. It is a close cousin to MAP in spirit, and the similarities rather than the differences should be emphasized.

von Weitzäcker's plan

Christian von Weitzäcker has proposed a plan that is also similar to MAP in many respects. Von Weitzäcker's plan would require firms to purchase permits to increase prices and would allow these permits to be traded freely.

However, like Howard's plan, this proposal differs from MAP both in its underlying theory and in its method of application. In the first place, von Weitzäcker's plan is concerned with *output* prices rather than input prices. The difference between stabilizing output prices (Net Sales per unit of *output*) and stabilizing input prices (Net Sales per unit of *input*) at first glance may seem to be merely an administrative matter, but it is more than that.[1]

Let's consider a firm that has experienced a large productivity gain without investment. Its costs per unit of output will be significantly decreased, and it will either maintain its original output and price or it will pass on the gain in lower prices so that it can sell permits. But under MAP, based on Net Sales per unit of *input,* the firm that experiences such a gain will have to pass it on in lower prices unless it buys additional Credit. If the firm maintains the same price and output while reducing inputs, it will *lose* Credit. This is because the property rights to Net Sales are determined by inputs in MAP (and represented by MAP Credit) but are determined by outputs in von Weitzäcker's proposal.

According to von Weitzäcker's plan, if the price of the permits is positive, a large influx of businesses would be expected to occur in areas where prices are decreasing merely to obtain permits. To provide an extreme example, we will say that transistor radios initially sold for $50. Then a new chip is discovered that reduces the price to $5. Since every radio produced entitles a firm to excess permits of $45, entry into the industry would be encouraged and the price of radios pushed down until it approached zero or possibly even became negative. In this way, an almost unlimited number of permits could be created that would hold down the measured price level— but only at the cost of the significant waste created by the overproduction of items undergoing technological advances. Under these circumstances it would even be profitable to produce and give away or dump unsaleable radios to obtain the permits earned, just as in socialist countries (where prices cannot be reduced below "cost") unsaleable goods have been produced and stored in warehouses to fulfill physical output production "norms." Von Weitzäcker's permits would be sold to producers who increased the prices of their goods, while the price index would be stabilized by the weight of the unsaleable, cheap radios.

As an alternative example, consider what happens if a firm invests heavily in research and development but produces no new technological breakthroughs. Under MAP, this firm would receive additional Credit; under von Weitzäcker's plan, it would receive no additional permits. MAP Credit is given for *investment* in productivity; von Weitzäcker's plan grants excess permits only for *actual increases* in productivity passed on in price reductions.

Von Weitzäcker's proposal also differs from MAP in the underlying theory. The intent of von Weitzäcker's plan is to make the price level adjust

---

[1] We believe that the use of Net Sales per unit of input is also preferable on administrative grounds. Output prices are far more difficult to control than input prices due to the large potential for quality variations that can substantially change the measure of the quantity of output.

automatically and instantly to the supply of money, so that the price level can be stabilized *indirectly* by controlling the money supply. MAP stabilizes the price level *directly*.

In von Weitzäcker's basic plan, the supply of permits varies directly with the money supply. This means that any increase in the money supply would immediately push up the quantity of permits, thereby forcing individual firms to raise their prices. This would eliminate the lag between monetary policy and inflation.

Von Weitzäcker designed the program in this manner because he believes that the *underlying* inflationary problem is the result of short-term political motivations on the part of government. He believes that if the government is made politically responsible for *immediate* increases in inflation caused by an increase in the money supply, it will be more likely to keep the money supply under control.

In our theory, the government *wants* to control inflation but cannot do so because decreases in aggregate demand result in unemployment. We have therefore established a *rule* that bases the increase in MAP Credit on the real growth rate in the economy. Monetary policy could be adjusted to such a rule without unleashing unemployment.

the "free market in money" proposals

Another set of proposals designed to use the market to solve inflation works in quite a different manner from MAP. This proposals include plans by F. von Hayek (1976) and Ben Klein (1975). Like von Weitzäcker, both von Hayek and Klein base their proposals on a political theory of inflation: inflation is the result of the government printing too much money. Their remedies, however, differ radically from von Weitzäcker's. Instead of instituting a program to make the government immediately responsible for any inflation that results from an increase in the money supply, von Hayek and Klein remove the government's monopoly over the money supply, leaving the issue of money to private firms. Von Hayek writes:

"It seems to me that if we could prevent governments from meddling with money, we would do more good than any government has ever done in this regard. And private enterprise would probably have done better than the best they have ever done."

There are three reasons why we do not believe that such a proposal would work. First, if anything is a natural monopoly, the money supply is. The transaction costs of a multi-currency society would be enormous. Second, the potential disruption of the system that could result from the failure of an important private money would deter the government from allowing any "money" to "go under." Finally, we would be fearful of charismatic individuals, who could secure the trust of and ruin a large number of people. A healthy fear of government excesses should be surpassed only by a fear of our own gullibility.

The reaction of such an economic downfall could be enormous. Even today, the FED finds it difficult to let an errant bank fail, as the case of Franklin National attests. Lenin once said that the best method of revolution was to debase the money supply. The von Hayek proposal, by easing a foreign country's ability to do that in spades, could be the yellow brick road to serfdom.

But even if national security were not an issue, we would still object to such a proposal on the basis of transaction costs. Conducting business in five or six currencies would be extremely costly. Every transaction would require a statement explaining what currency or basket of currencies was to be used as payment. Accounting procedures would be much more difficult, and the continuous monitoring of relative currency prices would be required to maintain trade. New "currencies" would always be developing, and sellers would have to decide which methods of payment to accept.

History also counsels against such a proposal. The early history of banking in the United States—replete with wildcat banks, multiple currencies, and continuous bankruptcies—leaves us more than a little doubtful about the success of the private control of money. A healthy democracy is composed of an intricate system of checks and balances both within government and between the government and the people. Leaving the regulation of the money supply to the public is too dangerous.

direct relativity bargaining

Another set of ideas that is very similar to MAP falls under the general heading of direct relativity bargaining and includes proposals by Adrian Wood (1978), Rueben Bellan (forthcoming), and Martin Bailey (1976). These proposals do not use the market to set relative prices, as MAP does; instead they employ existing bargaining procedures. Adrian Wood's proposal is the most developed. Under his plan, which operates only on wages, most of the existing apparatus of pay determination would be maintained, but the unit of account would be altered. Pay bargaining would not be accomplished in money terms; instead, it would be achieved directly in relative terms. Thus, the government would merely establish an infrastructure in which the bargaining could take place and leave the determination of relative pay to individual firms. This would mean that the government would set a national total for all wages and that the different groups of workers would bargain with each other as to how this given total would be shared.

The difficulty posed by this procedure is precisely how to establish this infrastructure. It would be impossible for all unions and managements to meet simultaneously to bargain, so presumably some accounting system would need to be developed that would facilitate the bargaining process. The ideal way to allow large numbers of disparate groups to bargain is to establish a market, in which case the Wood plan becomes similar to WIPP or Lerner's original market plan for wages. The problems this poses have already been discussed: controlling wages alone is unacceptable to labor.

Along the same lines—but in even less explicit form than Wood's plan—are the proposals by Bellan and Bailey. In Bellan's plan, all individuals would submit proposals to the government, which would then scale them down so that total wage settlements remained at 100 percent. In Bailey's plan, the government would set up a request control system, and all wage increases would be scaled back to a noninflationary level. Besides imposing regulation solely on wages (and therefore being unacceptable to labor), the problem with these proposals is the uncertainty about the degree of wage downscaling that would be required. On the one hand, expectational differences would result in different agreements about wages and prices, resulting in unjustifiable inequities and fear of commitment. On the other hand, if the uncertainty and expectational differences should be overcome (perhaps by insurance, indexing, coincidence, the convergence of expectations due to more accurate information, or coordination), the effectiveness of the plan would be lost entirely. Nothing would have changed except for the double unit of measurement (pre and post wage downscaling), and we would be back at square one.

There are probably many other proposals similar to MAP that we have not yet discovered. The underlying concept of MAP is too simple for variants of it not to have been proposed before. We believe that MAP is preferable to the plans we have mentioned here—perhaps only because we have incorporated in MAP many of the ideas of others who have worked along related lines. A continuous interchange of ideas should substantially improve all of these proposals.

the government's anti-inflation program

the direct government contribution

Until October 1978, it was difficult to tell whether or not the government had an anti-inflation program. Although whenever a project was not undertaken, it was called an inflationary project and innumerable appeals were made for everyone to join in the anti-inflation fight, it was merely a lot of talk and no action.

One of the reasons why there was no government approach to inflation was a lack of direct accountability and leadership. Our government is a heterogeneous group with many different viewpoints. In such a system, it understandably takes time for any group to take the initiative.

On October 24, 1978, President Carter filled the void with a wide-ranging anti-inflationary program consisting of what can best be called "selective mandatory voluntary controls" of wages and prices. This program consists of two sections: a direct anti-inflation contribution by the government, and government mobilization of the private sector's contribution. The following summary of the first section of this program is excerpted from the government's fact sheet.

The President has now acted:

(1) to intensify the anti-inflation efforts of government by:

—adopting a stringent budget policy that will create an overall climate in which the inflationary process can unwind,

—establishing procedures that minimize the inflationary impact of government regulations, and

—indicating his intention to veto legislative measures and other actions of government that provide benefits to narrow, special-interest groups;

(2) to break the upward spiral of costs and prices by:

—enunciating explicit numerical standards for noninflationary wage and price increases, and

87

—making clear his intention to use his administrative powers to support adherence to those standards in individual situations.

The burden of controlling inflation should not be left to monetary policy alone, which can only deal with the problem through tight restrictions on money and credit.

The President's new proposals for dealing with inflation constitute a balanced and concerted program under which tight budget restraint, private wage and price moderation, and responsible monetary policy support each other.

As the Executive Branch, Congress, and the private sector, working together, show sacrifice and restraint and we begin to make progress in reducing inflation, we should expect lower interest rates for consumers and businesses alike.

budgetary policy

The federal government must pursue a stringent budgetary policy with respect both to spending and to the budget deficit. The growth of spending must be strictly limited. As moderate and sustainable economic growth continues, the budget deficit must be reduced and eliminated. Business and labor must be convinced that excessive demands will not be created by the government's overall economic policies. Only under these circumstances will it be possible for inflationary pressures to unwind gradually.

To achieve this objective, it is neither necessary nor desirable to pursue a budgetary policy that seeks to wring inflation out of the economic system by raising unemployment. Attempting to reduce inflation by throwing millions of people out of work and idling a significant proportion of our plant facilities would be inequitable and intolerably costly. But the achievement of further overall reductions in unemployment will require that we show progress in reducing the rate of inflation.

In fiscal 1976, federal expenditures represented 22.5 percent of the nation's GNP and the deficit was $66 billion. Since then, the size of the deficit has been reduced substantially. In fiscal 1979, the deficit in the federal budget will be less than $40 billion. Next January, the Administration will submit its budget for fiscal 1980—the year beginning October 1, 1979. In the context of an overall economy growing at a moderate rate, the President has set targets for planning the 1980 budget under which

(1) the share of total spending in GNP would be reduced to

about 21 percent of GNP—a goal originally scheduled to be reached a year later—and

(2) the 1980 federal budget deficit would be reduced to less than half the level of 1976.

In order to contribute to these goals, the President has imposed severe limits on the hiring of federal employees for an indefinite period. Effective immediately, federal agencies may fill only one out of two vacancies as they occur. This step will reduce the number of federal employees budgeted for this fiscal year by about 20,000. In July, the President announced a 5.5 percent limitation on federal employee pay raises and a freeze on federal executive pay levels.

regulatory policy

During the last decade, we have expanded our efforts to protect the environment and the health and safety of workers and consumers. These goals are central to our welfare. But they are not free. Regulations designed to achieve these goals add to costs and hence to consumer prices. We must not abandon our regulatory goals, but we must attain them without imposing unnecessary burdens.

It is vital that equal attention be paid to decisions that impose costs on the public through raising private sector prices as to those [decisions] that involve the expenditure of funds through the budget.

With this principle in mind, the President has stated his intention personally to exercise his authority, as necessary, to ensure that the regulatory process is balanced and well managed, and that specific regulations with large economic impacts achieve their statutory goals at minimum economic cost and regulatory burden.

We are in full agreement with the general principles expressed in the President's program regarding the general characteristics of a successful anti-inflation program. We, too, are sure that "the burden of controlling inflation should not be left to monetary policy alone, which can only deal with the problem through tight restrictions on money and credit." Such a belief naturally complements the President's view that "attempting to reduce inflation by throwing millions of people out of work and idling a significant proportion of our plant facilities would be inequitable and intolerably costly." But we disagree with the follow-up statement that "the achievement of further overall reductions in unemployment will require that we show progress in reducing the rate of inflation." This means that in the fight against inflation, people should not lose their jobs but people who are unemployed now should remain unemployed. In our view, it is at least as intolerable and inequitable to keep an unemployed person unemployed as it is to fire an employed person. In either case, *unemployment should not be used as a tool to fight inflation.*

We certainly favor "a balanced and concerted program under which tight budget restraint, private wage and price moderation, and responsible monetary policy support each other." Unfortunately, the proposed measures show no promise of achieving the necessary cooperation between the various groups in society. The program fails to recognize how impossible it is for each of the three main groups—government, business, and labor—to make their required contributions unless it is certain that the other groups will also do their share.

Implicit in the very first of the President's principles—that spending policy alone cannot cure the inflation—is the recognition that our inflation is not the classical excess demand inflation due to "too much money chasing too few goods." Our problem is *not* that the public, together with government, is trying to buy more than our economy is able to produce. If this were the case, monetary restraint alone *would* be able to do the trick. It would remove the excess spending; no unemployment would result.

The President's call for coordination of wage and price moderation with monetary restraint implies a recognition that our inflation is primarily an *expectational* inflation in which total spending, prices, and wages are all rising in a vicious circle, compulsively trying to keep up with each other. The spell can be broken only by a simultaneous counter-inflationary pressure applied to all three of these factors. The President's program fails to provide this. Instead, it concentrates governmental efforts almost exclusively on total *spending.* Control of *prices* and *wages* is to be achieved by voluntary guidelines, appeals, prayers, occasional curses, and some threats of possibly illegal governmental discrimination against noncompliers.

Furthermore, instead of considering the *total spending in the economy* (of which government spending is only a part), the President's program concentrates primarily on the government's contribution to total spending as if the government deficit were the sole cause of increased total spending. This is a fundamental error—a confusion of thought. *Deficits do not cause inflation,* as we have carefully spelled out.

The government does have a special responsibility: only the government can stop the inflationary spiral. Government is after all the institution that is responsible for dealing with problems that affect society as a whole but are not automatically solved otherwise. Inflation is one of these problems.

the government as a victim of inflation

In an expectational inflation, the government is as much a *victim* of the vicious inflationary circle as business and labor. Government is forced to provide the increase in *spending* that is an essential ingredient in the inflationary process. The government will not be able to resist the pressure to increase spending as long as it continues to recognize that fighting inflation "by throwing millions of people out of work" is not only "inequitable and intolerably costly" but also futile, because it is a policy that no democratic government can complete.

The belief that government deficits cause inflation produces severe guilt feelings in the government. This may explain why the part played by increasing government spending in the tripartite inflationary process is over-stressed and suggests that the contributions required of the other two victim-culprits toward moderating (or curing) the inflation are secondary. It may also explain why the government punishes itself by imposing arbitrary "anti-inflationary" restrictions on its operations or by promising to compensate for its sins by being more efficient or more equitable. Thus, the President sets a number of arbitrary "targets"—to cut the budget deficit in half, to reduce the government share of GNP to 21 percent, to impose "severe limits on hiring" (allowing federal agencies to fill only one out of every two vacancies), and to set a discriminatory 5.5 percent pay-raise limitation on government salaries.

These are not anti-inflation targets at all. They are proposals that may or may not be warranted on the basis of equity or efficiency considerations, but that should be decided independently of the fight against inflation. If warranted, the proposals should be adopted, and if not, they should be rejected—inflation or no inflation. If the government's share in national economic activity should be reduced, it should be reduced even if there is no inflation. If the number of federal employees should be cut, it should be cut even if there is no inflation. (If arbitrary overall cuts can be made without significantly impeding efficiency, they should be made even more rapidly. Setting arbitrary rules is merely a cover for poor management.)

These same arguments hold for a number of other impeccable principles of sound government policy stated in the President's program, such as "We must not abandon our regulatory goals, but we must attain them without imposing unnecessary burdens" or the "intention to veto legislative measures . . . that provide benefits to narrow, special-interest groups." If a regulation is unwarranted in an inflationary context, it is also unwarranted if there is no inflation. If a special-interest bill should be vetoed in an inflationary situation, it should also be vetoed in a noninflationary situation. These are issues of efficiency in government, not anti-inflation issues. The government *is* inefficient, just as many private firms are inefficient, but it was inefficient even when there was no inflation problem. Issues of equity and efficiency only distract attention from our inflation problem and lead to confusion. MAP—by focusing attention on the essence of inflation—separates such issues from the inflation problem and allows each issue to be dealt with on the basis of its own merits.

government mobilization of the private sector's contribution

The second part of the President's anti-inflation program is directed at the private sector. The following summary is excerpted from the government's fact sheet.

Government must take the lead in the effort to slow inflation. Actions by government alone, however, will not suffice. A successful campaign to break the continuing cycle by which wage and price increases feed upon one another will require restraint on the part of everyone. A voluntary approach to achieve this goal must reflect several basic principles:

(1) It must be equitable.

(2) It must establish clear and explicit standards for both wage and price behavior.

(3) It must instill confidence that others will participate.

The government must set its own house in order, and it must take measures to encourage individual decision makers in the private sector to do likewise.

price/wage standards for 1979

The President has asked for a stronger effort by the private sector to be achieved by (1) instituting an explicit numerical standard for wage and fringe-benefit increases; (2) specifying a price deceleration standard for individual firms in a fashion that is consistent with the limitation on wage increases; (3) expanding the government's efforts to monitor inflation trends and to identify sectors of the economy where the standards are being exceeded; and (4) instituting specific government measures to encourage compliance with the standards.

It is essential that these more explicit standards for private wage and price decisions retain the flexibility required for equity and economic efficiency. The following standards, promulgated by the President, accomplish that objective:

wage standards

Annual **increases in wages** and **private fringe-benefit** payments **should not exceed 7 percent.** This standard is achievable and consistent with protecting the real incomes of workers against inflation.

In new collective-bargaining situations, a contract in which wage and fringe-benefit increases average no more than 7 percent annually over the life of the contract will be consistent with the pay standard. However, no more than an 8-percent pay increase should be included within the first year of a multi-year contract.

In the interest of equity or improved productivity, some exemptions from the pay limitation are allowed. First, workers who earn an hourly wage below $4.00 are excluded from the program. Second, wage increases in excess of the standard are acceptable if they reflect explicit changes in work rules and practices that result in demonstrable improvements in productivity of equal or greater value. Third, wage increases above the standard are justifiable if required in order to maintain a close, historical, tandem relationship to another employee group whose wage adjustment occurred prior to the announcement of the program.

price standards

A single standard for individual firms' price increases would be impractical. . . . But the standard for prices must be as explicit as that for wages.

The price standard requires that **individual firms limit their cumulative price increases over the next year to one-half of a percentage point below the firm's average annual rate of price increase during 1976–1977.**

The 1976–1977 period has been selected as being representative of basic underlying cost and productivity trends in individual industries. Some industries experienced abnormally high rates of price increase during that period. These extremes are taken into account by limiting the price increase for an individual firm to no more than 9.5 percent.

Furthermore, if hourly wage-rate increases within a firm decelerate by more than one-half of a percentage point relative to the 1976–1977 rate of increase, the deceleration of prices should be commensurately tightened to reflect a full passthrough into prices of the moderation of wage increases.

Firms that cannot meet the deceleration standard because of uncontrollable cost increases will be required to show that their before-tax profit margin (on sales) is no higher than the average of the firm's best two out of three fiscal years ending prior to October 1, 1978.

a program of "real wage insurance"

(1) Groups of employees would become eligible for the program through certification by their employer that their wage increase over the next year falls within the 7-percent standard outlined above.

(2) Members of employee groups that meet the standard would receive a tax refund if the consumer price index (CPI) increased by more than 7 percent over the year.

(3) That refund would be equal to the excess of the CPI increase over 7 percent applied to the employee's wages, up
to some reasonable limit.

Widespread observation of the standard should lead to a rate of
inflation below 7 percent. But this is an uncertain world and
there are risks for those who cooperate. By substantially
eliminating those risks, the real wage insurance program will
provide a strong incentive to observe the standards and a
major support for the fight against inflation.

incentives for compliance

This is a voluntary program. Nevertheless, individuals and
firms cannot be expected to adhere to the suggested limitations
on prices and wages unless they are provided with a reasonable expectation that others will do the same. Thus, government must be prepared to support the standards through its
own actions. In this respect, the Administration will interpret
wage or price increases above the standards as an indication
of inflationary conditions in the markets concerned— shortages, excessive market power, shelter from competition,
etc.—and the Administration is prepared to take those steps
within its power to alleviate such conditions. The range of
potential actions would include the following:

(1) A reexamination of various restrictions on import competition in industries in which wage or price increases are
exceeding the standards, and, where administratively possible, relaxing these barriers to trade. Many of these restrictions have the objective of protecting the output and
employment of domestic industries. But they are not intended to provide an umbrella under which excessive price
and cost increases could be imposed on the American
public.

(2) A request to the appropriate regulatory agencies that they,
in their decisions on rates and entry, evaluate the reasonableness of cost-passthrough and other rate-increase
requests in light of the anti-inflation standards for wage
and price behavior.

(3) An examination of specific markets in which minimum
levels for prices or wages are set by administrative regulations. Those regulations will be modified if inflationary
pressures and nonobservance of the standards are evident.

(4) The circumstances surrounding specific inflationary situations will be brought to the public's attention through
public hearings and reports of the Council on Wage and

Price Stability. The public can help by redirecting their purchases away from those markets where inflationary pressures are evident.

In effect, increases in excess of the standards will trigger a consideration of government policies and programs that affect the specific market in which the excessive increase takes place. Most of the actions outlined above can be adopted administratively (i.e., no legislation is required). In other cases, the Administration will be prepared to provide the Congress with specific legislative proposals if necessary to change government policies that exacerbate individual inflationary situations.

government as a buyer

The federal government itself is a major purchaser of goods and services. By channeling its procurement to those firms whose price and wage decisions meet the standards of noninflationary behavior, the government, acting as a prudent buyer, can realize important long-term savings in its procurement budget and simultaneously take the lead in the fight against inflation.

We agree wholeheartedly with the three basic principles that the Carter Administration has presented as fundamental to a campaign that will successfully break the continuing inflationary process. Such a campaign must be equitable; it must establish clear and explicit standards for both wage and price behavior, and must instill confidence that others will comply with the standards. But the President's program scores low marks on precisely these standards.

the wage standard

The use of wage standards that differ from the standards for other types of income is an obvious infringement of the equity criteria. So, too, is the authorization of wage increases above the standard "to maintain a historical tandem relationship with other wages." Such a policy would merely encourage more and more claims of historical tandem relationships.

Emphasis on wage income has led to the downfall of every previous incomes policy. Such emphasis is misplaced on all criteria—ethical, administrative, and political. *All* costs—payments for *all* productive factors—contribute to inflation; no factor should be singled out for more stringent treatment.

Differentiating between income groups also contributes greatly to making an incomes policy unmanageable. The administrative and political difficulties multiply enormously as the number of affected relative shares increases. In addition to showing that the policy on the whole is fair, it becomes

96

necessary to persuade every group that it is being treated fairly with respect to each one of the other groups.

the price standard

The government's price standard is completely indefensible. To suggest that individual firms should limit their cumulative price increases over the next year to one-half of a percentage point below the firm's average annual rate of price increase during 1976–1977 is arbitrary and unfair. Firms that held down their rate of price increase during these periods would be penalized even though they may have held down their prices to help in the inflation crisis. Thus, the President's program penalizes the "good guys."

The alternative profit margin limitation for firms that are exempted from the price guideline on account of "uncontrollable costs" is similarly faulty.

the problem of compliance

One of our greatest concerns is the government's method of inducing compliance. The program is said to be voluntary. However, the government states that it must be prepared to support the standards by government actions. Because these actions affect different people in different ways, compliance becomes voluntary for some and nonvoluntary for others.

This method of achieving compliance leaves many unanswered questions. The government suggests that it will reexamine various restrictions on import competition if firms do not adhere to the standards. Does this mean that if firms do follow the standards, the government won't? Reexamination of restrictions on import competition is called for *at all times;* if import restrictions are no longer necessary, they should be removed whether guidelines are being followed or not. The same applies to regulatory reform. Again, this demonstrates the confusion that follows from combining two conceptually different programs into one.

Enforcement by public hearing presents another problem. It makes government an arm-chair quarterback, second-guessing all decisions made in all markets. This can only lead to administrative complexities, political difficulties, and an ultimate breakdown of either the market or the government's program.

Using government procurement as a means of enforcement is subject to these same criticisms. The government would have to refuse to buy from least-cost suppliers, thereby increasing costs and contributing not only to government inefficiency but to inflation as well.

Underlying all of these unfortunate inequities and inefficiencies is the recognition that simply fixing all wage and price increases at the magic figure of 7 percent (or any other figure) will not work. The resulting freeze of relative prices and income relationships would destroy the flexibility of our market-based economy in dealing with continually changing tastes, techniques, and availabilities. All the irregularities, the discriminations, the inequities, and the interferences we have been criticizing are basically attempts to provide *holes* in the otherwise complete encapsulation of the economy—holes through which the economy should breathe.

Clearly discernible behind all the deviations from a completely equitable uniform freeze is a recognition that what we really want to stabilize is not the *actual* rate of increase of every price (at 7 percent or zero or any other norm) but only the *average* price. Thus, some prices would be permitted to rise above the norm and others to fall below it, thereby guiding the essential changes in the use of resources in a living economy.

But this objective cannot be reached because the government has no theory of how all *actual* individual prices and wages can be left free to adjust to the myriad changes in economic conditions even while the *average* price is stabilized. In the absence of such a theory, it can only resort to an "ad-hoc-ery" of the miscellaneous administrative measures. Government is nakedly in need of a theory and a program to implement that theory and to carry out the policy it has enunciated. MAP supplies both the theory and the program.

The theory of MAP distinguishes between what the government itself can do and what it can induce business and labor to do. The MAP program provides the mechanism by which the government can ensure that business and labor will provide the required cooperation.

The basic anti-inflation problem is to stop (or slow) the vicious circle that compels business, labor, and government to increase wages, prices, and total spending, respectively, to keep up with each other in the tripartite expectational inflation race. MAP *directly* eliminates the compulsions of business and labor to increase prices and wages. It thereby *indirectly* eliminates the pressure on the government to increase total spending.

The MAP disincentive smoothly and continuously performs all the tasks that the government's "persuasions" can accomplish, at best, only sporadically and unevenly. By freely permitting *actual* Net Sales to depart from the national *average* increase in Net Sales (if accompanied by the purchase or sale of MAP "Credit"), MAP makes completely unnecessary all the discriminatory, inequitable, and arbitrary "exceptions" directed in the government's program toward loosening the straightjacket on the economy.

real wage insurance

One novel part of the government's program is Real Wage Insurance, which was designed to make the overall program more attractive to labor—perhaps to compensate for placing the most stringent restraint on wages. Although it was quickly abandoned, Real Wage Insurance is worth examining here, if only very briefly, as a striking example of the dangers of promoting a program—making it appear more attractive than it is—at the expense of its effectiveness in achieving the primary purpose.

The Real Wage Insurance Program was designed to provide an incentive to workers to hold down their wage increase demands. But it did a poor job. It provided very large compensations for very small contributions toward the anti-inflation goal. In fact, many workers and employers who contributed nothing at all to the anti-inflation effort were compensated.

This group included all workers who were unable to obtain wage increases above 7 percent or who expected the price increase to be less than

7 percent. They had no incentive to reduce their wage demands, although they would have been compensated for price increases in excess of 7 percent. Workers who expected the price increase to be more than 7 percent and to receive a still greater wage increase would have suffered by complying with the standard. They, too, were offered no incentive to moderate their wage demands.

Only workers who expected prices to rise more than 7 percent but who were only able to obtain wage increases *between 7 percent and the expected price rise* would have responded to the plan. To maintain their real wages, they would have had to petition their employers to reduce their wage increases to just 7 percent. The government would then have paid the workers the foregone wages *plus* the required additional wages to make their pay rise commensurate with the price rise. The contribution to disinflation would consist entirely of the substitution of the government's payment for the employers' payment of the foregone wages.

Incidentally, MAP—while applying equal disincentives for *all* wage and price increases—contains a much more satisfactory element of real income protection. In the payments for MAP Credit, which continue as long as the inflationary pressure continues, firms with above-norm wage and profit increases provide compensation to firms with below-norm wage and profit increases.

no real sacrifice is required

There is one more quite general comment that we feel compelled to make about the tone of the whole government's approach to securing the cooperation of business and labor in the essential simultaneous slowing (and stopping) of the tripartite vicious circle of expectational inflation. The government repeatedly calls for restraint and sacrifice by all parties and leads the way by arbitrarily cutting its own activities and its own employment of the nation's productive resources. Would the appropriate response to the government's appeal be for the rest of the country to reduce their activities and their employment of productive resources in the same way? If so, this would result in precisely the "throwing of millions of people out of work and idling a significant proportion of our plant and facilities" that the government has pronounced inequitable, intolerable, and unnecessary. Such a sacrifice is surely not what the government has in mind. Indeed, there is no need for any economic sacrifice at all, unless we believe—as many do, but the government expressly denies—that we must use increased unemployment "to wring inflation out of the economic system."

On the contrary, as the inflation weakens (even before it is completely stopped), the diminished fear of accelerating inflation could make it safer to engage in expansionary policies that would increase employment and productive output instead of prices. Rather than making a sacrifice, we would profit from increased employment, output, investment, and consumption. The call for sacrifice is a mistake.

Nor does the word "restraint" best describe what is intended. It is, of course, essential that business and labor *cooperate* in any successful anti-inflation program. Restraint *is* required in the raising of money prices and money wages. Once prices and wages stop rising, the excessive increase in total spending (and money) can diminish, but this is not a *restraint* in the sense of being the effective force in restraining the inflationary process. It is *a response to* the elimination of the pressure on the government to increase spending to keep up with rising prices, not *the cause of* the reduced increase in prices and wages. The reduction in the increase in total spending does not imply any reduction of real output, economic activity, employment, or real income. These may increase—rather than decrease, as the government's examples might suggest.

There will, of course, probably be an irresistible temptation for the more enthusiastic monetarists to claim that the reduced increase in the money supply (and total spending) was the "basic" or "ultimate" cause of the improvement. But identical claims will also be made by business on behalf of their restraint in raising prices and by labor on behalf of their restraint in raising wages. Not one of these three claims can stand alone. Just as the ongoing inflation forced all three to run fast in the race to keep up with each other, so does the cooperation between MAP and sound finance enable each sector to slow down as the other two slow down. The credit goes to the cooperation.

business' anti-inflation program

a summary of the business program

Business' position on inflation has often been characterized as "the old-time religion." The following extracts from a letter sent by the Chamber of Commerce of the United States to President Carter on October 12, 1978, express the Chamber's views on how best to reduce inflation and provide insight into "the old-time religion."

The National Chamber and the Gallup Organization recently surveyed 1,100 American business leaders, representing firms of all sizes, industries, and regions of the country, to obtain their assessment of the major causes of inflation:

1st *Excessive federal government deficits and accommodating growth of money supply*

2nd *Costly federal regulations*

3rd *Taxes that discourage productivity-increasing investment and research and development*

4th *Some large, bargaining-unit-negotiated wage increases*

5th *Social Security tax increases*

6th *Federal minimum wage increases*

7th *Federal farm price support increases*

8th *U.S. dollar decline abroad*

9th *Nonunion wage increases*

10th *Unemployment insurance taxes*

11th *Interest rate increases*

12th *Workmen's compensation increases*

Most of these causes of inflation can be modified by changes in federal government policies, and we are aware of your efforts to reduce some inflationary public policies. However, as you well know, much more must be done to reduce inflation, and we recommend the following public policies to dampen inflation during 1979 and 1980:

(1) Slow down the nearly double-digit growth of federal spending that is occurring during 1978 to less than $35 billion for fiscal year 1980.

(2) Slow down the double-digit 14 percent growth of federal taxes that is occurring during 1978 and provide tax relief of at least $25 billion for FY 1980.

(3) Reduce the federal deficit to $25 billion for FY 1980 and achieve a balanced budget by FY 1982 with high employment.

(4) Encourage the Federal Reserve to stay within its targets for the growth of money, instead of continuing with the excessive growth experienced during the last 18 months, which is, unfortunately, leading to the tightening of money and consequently higher interest rates.

(5) Slow down the growth of federal regulations by placing a freeze on regulatory budgets and personnel for FY 1980, strengthen and enforce E.O. 12044 by requiring calculations of regulatory costs and benefits and a credible central government review, and require that new regulations be implemented only if old regulations of at least equal cost are removed. Based on historical data, limiting the growth of regulations could reduce price inflation by 0.5 percent in 1979 and 1980.

(6) Defer increases in the federal minimum wage as recommended by Federal Reserve Chairman G. William Miller. Applying the studies of Professor Jacob Mincer of Columbia University and Professor George S. Tolley and colleagues of the University of Chicago, a two-year deferral could reduce consumer prices by 1.6 percent; a one-year deferral, by 0.8 percent; exclusion of young workers from the increase until a 15 percent youth differential is provided could reduce consumer prices by 0.6 percent and create 400,000 jobs for minority and other youth.

(7) Defer 1979 and 1980 increases in Social Security taxes enacted during 1977 by requiring federal personnel to pay Social Security taxes, as nearly all other workers and employers in America must do. The federal employees' tax payments would offset the deferred Social Security tax increases and bring down consumer prices by as much as 0.33 percent during 1979 and 0.5 percent during 1980.

(8) *Repeal or modify the Davis–Bacon Act and change its administration to reduce wage and price inflation caused by prevailing wage requirements.*

(9) *Review federal personnel compensation and bring it into true comparability with personnel compensation in state and local government and industry. According to the Commerce Department, average federal civilian pay in 1977 was 42 percent higher than average pay in state and local government or industry ($17,404, compared to $12,230 and $12,244). Steps toward true pay comparability could help reduce wage and thereby price inflation by 0.25 percent.*

(10) *Restrain excessive sugar and other farm price supports.*

(11) *Encourage investment in modern tools and equipment and structures for American workers, such as by ensuring that capital depreciation allowances are equal to replacement costs in 1980.*

(12) *Establish a cooperative effort with labor, management, and government to encourage productivity improvement throughout the economy.*

(13) *Establish a meaningful federal effort to achieve productivity improvement in the federal government workplace.*

(14) *Encourage the Organization for Petroleum Exporting Countries to maintain current crude oil prices; the rumored 5- to 10-percent increase in crude oil prices could increase U.S. consumer prices by 0.5 percent.*

(15) *Adopt policies and programs to strengthen America's competitiveness in world markets; vigorous support is needed to stimulate job-creating exports and investment transactions.*

(16) *Encourage U.S. trading partners to maintain healthy growing economies and to seek reduction in barriers to trade in the Multilateral Trade Negotiations, both of which would help to increase U.S. exports.*

We wholeheartedly support these recommendations to cure the real causes of inflation. More importantly, according to answers to a questionnaire sent to all Congressional candidates, a majority of the House of Representatives in 1979 and 1980 would support fighting the real causes of inflation that we have identified.

Your advisers argue that placing a straitjacket on the entire private economy for several years is necessary to restrain a few collective bargaining settlements. We recommend against such overkill and suggest dealing selectively with the few inflationary settlements or excessive price increases as they occur.

Despite the unsuccessful wage and price control experience of 1970–1974 in the United States, the undesirable consequences of controls do not appear to be fully appreciated. Controls create domestic shortages. Controls encourage unwanted changes in product quality. Controls require wasteful form-filling and reporting. Controls require knowledge that is unavailable; consequently, they necessarily fail to account for the huge variations in economic conditions between different industries. They interrupt the allocative function of prices in a free society.

Because wage and price increases are symptoms of inflation and not major causes and because of the difficulties of managing a fair, effective, and democratic program, it is no wonder that wage and price controls are usually judged useless or positively harmful. Even the few analysts who detect some good in controls estimate only small, short-term improvements at best and readily admit that even these improvements disappear in time.

American business people, workers, and consumers are the victims—not the cause—of inflation. Rather than placing controls on the symptoms of inflation, controls should be placed on the double-digit growth of federal taxes, spending, and regulations, such as a 7 percent limit on the increase in federal taxes, a 5.75 percent increase in overall federal spending, and a freeze on net new regulations.

We think it is fair to summarize business' position on inflation as follows: 90 percent of the inflation can be attributed to government. Its unsound fiscal and monetary practices, the increased taxes levied on business to finance expanded government activities, and its regulation of economic activities have pushed up costs and prices. These are the primary causes of inflation. The other 10 percent can be attributed to unreasonable demands for increased wages, which have increased costs and set an inflationary spiral in motion that has trapped business in the middle and forced firms to raise prices.

We agree with many of the Chamber of Commerce's criticisms of government policies—but mainly for reasons that are not relevant to the inflation problem. Nearly all the positive policies recommended by the Chamber contain elements that would contribute to any successful anti-inflation program. But unless these policies also contain other elements, which are missing or even explicitly or implicitly rejected in the Chamber's 1978 statement, the program is bound to fail.

some general comments

Of the 16 measures recommended by the Chamber, 1, 3, 9, 10, and 13 are closely related to reducing the government deficit, either by explicitly or implicitly calling for reductions in federal spending. All of these items are related to the view widely held in business circles that central to the government's 90-percent responsibility for inflation is its indulgence in deficits instead of balancing its budget. It seems almost to be held as an axiom that there is a direct relationship between government deficits and inflation. As we have said before, we think this is a fundamental error—a confusion of thought. Deficits do not cause inflation, even though they may constitute a part of excessive total spending.

The Chamber assumes that the government is strong enough to be able, by a restrictive monetary and fiscal policy, to create enough unemployment and a sufficiently severe credit crunch to force labor and business to stop their wage and price increases. This means that government must somehow overcome the humanitarian, political, and financial pressures to increase spending to keep up with wage and price increases—and even withstand the dangers of riot, revolution, and electoral defeat—pressures that until now have compelled government to participate in the inflationary circle. In our view, the political realities will not allow a depression to be imposed that is sufficiently strong to stop the inflation. Many businesspeople agree with this assessment, but then they shift to the completely different proposition that none of the present troubles would ever have arisen if the government had consistently followed a "sound monetary policy." This is hard to disprove—or indeed to prove. But even if it were *known* to be true, it does not indicate what action the government should take in the present situation—and, after all, that is where we are.

MAP recognizes the present existence of the vicious circle of the expectational inflation and *simultaneously removes all the compulsions* that perpetuate the inflation. This enables the government to apply functional finance—to use increases and decreases in total spending (and the money supply) as a tool for preventing inflation and depression.

The emphasis of much of the business community on the role of the money supply in inflation is perfectly justified. But only MAP, by imposing the restraint directly on money incomes instead of indirectly via unemployment and the credit crunch, can provide a means for reaching the monetary goal instead of just talking about it. Moreover, MAP provides a gauge that indicates more precisely when more deficit or more surplus is needed. MAP will therefore make it much easier for the government to run the type of policy that business and all reasonable individuals demand.

MAP also ensures that government enterprises are treated in the same way as private enterprises. Since governmental bodies will have to buy extra MAP Credit whenever they generate excess income per unit of input, they will thereby offset any inflationary impact of their activities. This control becomes stronger as the economy approaches capacity constraints, and it is far more even-handed than popular referendum reactions such as California's Proposition 13. MAP forces government agencies, as well as all other components of society, to recognize and to respond to that basic economic proposition. There is no such thing as a free lunch.

some specific comments

Thus far in this chapter, we have been considering government spending policy, at which the main thrust of the business criticism is directed. But when we come to business' specific anti-inflation proposals, we find that 14 of their 16 "public policies to dampen inflation" are directed at lowering particular expenditures or particular costs and prices. The underlying theory behind this approach is that if costs are reduced or particular expenditures are cut out, inflation will be slowed. This underlying theory is wrong. Reducing either costs or spending lowers the current *level* of without affecting the *rate of increase* in costs or expenditures.

A decrease in costs will only provide a one-time reduction in price. After it is achieved, the inflation will continue. A cost decrease will not provide the continuing offset needed to diminish the rate of inflation. Similarly, a one-time reduction in spending will not provide the reduction in the *rate of increase* in spending required to diminish the rate of inflation.

There is a situation in which a one-time reduction in costs and in price can help cure the inflation. This would occur if the reduction in price had the effect of lowering the expectations of future price increases. However, the Chamber's particular proposals affect too small a percentage of the total economy to make a meaningful dent in inflationary expectations.

Only after the inflation problem has been solved by the integration of MAP with functional finance can these lesser (but not unimportant) related issues be rationally decided on their own ground. Such questions of efficiency of federal regulation (item 5 of the measures recommended by the Chamber) should be decided in their own right and not on the basis of their inflationary impact. If a regulation is not cost effective, it is not cost effective in a noninflationary economy or an inflationary economy. To say that we should curb regulation to slow inflation implies that we should not curb regulation if we had no inflation. This is hardly a strong enough condemnation of unjustified regulation. This same argument applies to all the other points in the Chamber's list.

The only exception is recommendation 4 pertaining to the Federal Reserve. In the absence of MAP, the Federal Reserve is unable to "stay within its targets for the growth of money." It is compelled to increase this supply to provide the government's ante in the expectational inflation races. With MAP, a modest modification (or perhaps only a clarification) of this target would enable the Federal Reserve to collaborate with the government in playing the Functional Finance Game. And MAP's inside tips on when increases or decreases in total spending are required would help them play more successfully.

We reiterate that the federal minimum wage is not of fundamental relevance to inflation. At best, its elimination would provide a once-and-for-all lowering of the price level.

Productivity is of fundamental importance to our society. But it is not relevant for inflation. Even if productivity were increasing at 10 percent a year, inflation could be raging at 15 or 20 percent, just as it could if there were no growth in productivity.

The Chamber's assessment of some recent wage settlements seems to reflect the common belief that particular higher wage increases are justified by increases in *technical* productivity. This rule holds only to the degree that the technical progress increases the equilibrium wage for the workers in question—but technical progress can *decrease* the equilibrium wage. The benefit from technical progress consists of the cheapening of the product and the possible setting free of resources for other uses. Exploiting this rule by applying it independently of the *market* creates inflationary pressure for the "equalization up" of other wages.

Measures for maintaining a sound tax base for the Social Security system (item 7 of the Chamber's recommendations), for increasing productivity in government (item 13), for increasing productivity in general (item 11), and for reducing monopolistic practices (item 8) all contribute to increasing national productivity. MAP also increases productivity, although indirectly. Productivity takes investment and hard work. In an inflationary economy, a return to investment is often hampered by economic uncertainties. By establishing a stable price level, MAP increases the reliability of the rewards for hard work and investment. But measures to increase productivity should not be confused with measures for curing inflation.

Asking OPEC not to raise crude oil prices (item 14) is harmless, but even if it should work, it is still a once-and-for-all measure and not part of an anti-inflation policy. A successful U.S. anti-inflation policy cannot be imposed on foreigners. Only we can solve our inflation problem.

We agree with the position of the Chamber of Commerce that the guidelines proposed by the President are not the answer to our current inflation problem and in some cases are equivalent to the worst type of controls. We do not believe, however, that the selective enforcement of the few restrictions that the Chamber has suggested is a viable alternative policy, because it would be wasteful and unfair to the industries, unions, and government services that would be singled out for costly restraints.

Nevertheless, we believe we are in sympathy with the Chamber's concerns. The business sector's fear of mandatory and comprehensive wage and price controls is well founded. Such controls would mark the beginning of the end of our economic system as we now know it. Only the firms themselves have the necessary knowledge to determine the proper prices. This is why MAP does nothing more than add its overall anti-inflationary incentive to all the other influences on the determination of prices and wages.

MAP breaks the vicious inflationary circle in which everyone is a victim. It stabilizes the price level and frees the government to maintain a sound monetary and fiscal policy, with neither excessive nor insufficient total spending in the economy.

14

labor's anti-inflation program

a summary of labor's program

Labor is, of course, an extremely heterogeneous group. It is composed of numerous collective-bargaining units of differing degrees of strength. Much of labor is nonunionized. Still, when we speak about "labor," we generally are referring to the unionized sector, which sets the standards for the nonunionized sectors. In some cases, nonunion employers observe union settlements and duplicate them or even improve on them to keep their employees from forming or joining a union. Organized labor's position on an anti-inflation proposal is therefore a reliable barometer of the position of the entire labor sector.

The AFL–CIO is concerned about inflation. The organization's comments on President Carter's proposal in an October 31, 1978 pamphlet follow.

anti-inflation program

The AFL–CIO Executive Council agrees with President Carter's conclusion that inflation is the nation's No. 1 problem; supports his determination that prompt, remedial action must be taken; and concurs with his contention that austerity must be shared equally by all Americans.

Time and time again we have pointed out that the American worker and particularly those living on fixed-income retirement benefits are the chief victims of inflation.

The last few years, the sad but incontrovertible fact is that the real income of working people has been reduced and each additional week brings additional distress to America's working families and retirees.

So it is with reluctance that we find the program devised by the President's economic advisers to be inequitable and unfair.

It proposes budgetary cuts which could increase unemploy-

107

ment. It threatens continuation of regulatory actions designed to protect workers, the environment, and the economy.

It does not protect consumers from runaway price increases for the four necessities of life—food, energy, housing, and medical care—the areas where inflation hits hardest.

The program excludes, for all practical purposes, all sources of income except wages.

The price guideline is so flexible as to be nonexistent and is without effective enforcement. It allows those who raised prices the most in the past two years to profit further from that conduct.

The wage controls are inflexible and not voluntary and will be eagerly enforced by every public and private employer in the land and by the IRS and by threats of blacklisting and official denunciation.

The wage-control figure for federal workers, set at 1.5 percent below the control figure for all other workers, is clearly discriminatory.

There is no provision whatsoever for control of profits or interest rates, now rapidly approaching all-time highs and endangering the entire economy and particularly the housing industry.

Dividends, capital gains, unearned income from tax shelters—all are completely free to climb without limit. Commodity speculators remain free to drive up the prices of food and other raw materials. Banks and other financial institutions remain free to speculate at will against the American dollar. Professional fees are not effectively controlled, and there is no mechanism for halting rapid increases in rents.

There is no mechanism for adjustment of inequities caused by wage controls. The low-wage exemption of the Nixon Pay Board, mandated by Congress, was far more equitable. That figure, exempting the working poor, was $3.50 an hour. Using the same formula today, the low-wage exemption would be $5.50 an hour, not the $4.00 the President decreed.

The decision to include all fringe-benefit costs in the wage-control figure is simply impractical. Government-mandated costs for pensions, for example, will reduce the wage portion of the package far below the figure needed to catch up with living cost increases alone.

The so-called "Real Wage Insurance" is vague, details are nonexistent, and the legislative route is so unpredictable that *we cannot honestly tell our members that they would have the protection the President promised.*

This Executive Council does not determine the collective-bargaining goals of the affiliated unions. In the final analysis, the members of the 60,000 public- and private-sector collective-bargaining units that will negotiate contracts over the next year must determine for themselves what they need to provide food, housing, energy, and medical care for their families. In making their decision, they will consider the costs of all the necessities they must provide for their families and the profitability of their employer.

When they read of the adverse reaction to the President's program as reflected in the continued devaluation of the dollar and observe the continued rapid rise in the costs of food, housing, and medical care, and the additional profits for energy companies that will follow adoption of the natural-gas deregulation bill, they certainly will not feel confident that others are equal partners in austerity.

While the program demonstrates the President's desires to address the problem of inflation, the plan his advisers have devised is unfair and inequitable and the end result of their ill-considered proposals could well be another recession, with mass unemployment, which at least one Administration spokesman is already predicting.

Since another recession, with mass unemployment and widespread suffering, is unthinkable and since the President's economic advisers have so far rebuffed suggestions for changes to make this third anti-inflation program more equitable, we now believe the time has come for mandatory, legislated, economic controls.

We do not like controls. We do not welcome government operation of the marketplace. But recession is worse; runaway inflation is worse; the discriminatory application of wage controls is worse; the distorting of laws for purposes other than those intended is worse; public scapegoating without due process is worse.

Therefore, we urge the President to draft a legislative program of full economic controls, covering every source of income—profits, dividends, rents, interest rates, executive compensation, and professional fees, as well as wages and prices.

It is our belief that this matter is of such urgency that the President should call a special session of the Congress for the development of a full and fair controls program. Such a pro-

gram should be detailed—not a standby grant of unspecified authority to the President. It must be a program that treats all Americans equally, provides a prompt and proper mechanism for the adjustment of inequities, controls prices for everything, and lasts only for the duration of the emergency. Such a full, legislated, economic control program has now become the only responsible method for halting this inflation.

Since we believe the Administration is already headed in the direction of overall controls in piecemeal and ill-designed stages, America might as well do it right and do it now. That means legislative action must be prompt, the mechanism fair and effective, and the sacrifice equal.

If these criteria are met in a legislated controls program, such a program would have our support.

Overall, we find labor's statements about the government's anti-inflation program reasonable. However, we disagree with some of labor's comments, and we find some more commendable than others. Dividing these comments into general categories, we find two areas of concern: (1) equity concerns, and (2) efficiency concerns.

equity concerns

These concerns refer to a number of different kinds of equity. The most significant is the concern about equity among different types of income. This theme continually reappears throughout labor's program. For example, labor charges "that the program excludes, for all practical purposes, all sources of income except wages." A later complaint is that "There is no provision whatsoever for control of profits or interest rates. . . . Dividends, capital gains, unearned income from tax shelters—all are completely free to climb without limit." Labor concludes that "the members of the 60,000 public- and private-sector collective-bargaining units . . . certainly will not feel confident that others are equal partners in austerity" or that the government's proposals conform to President Carter's contention that "austerity must be shared equally by all Americans."

By treating all income equally, MAP eliminates the grounds for any of these complaints. By applying its counter-inflationary incentive to Net Sales per unit of input, MAP works on dividends, capital gains, profits, interest rates, and all other forms of income in exactly the same ways that it works on wages. MAP reminds everybody that there is always exactly 100 percent of the pie to go around and leaves the division of the national income among firms to the market and the division within each firm to the collective-bargaining process so deeply embedded in our American economic system.

The second equity concern is labor's conviction that unemployment should not be used to fight inflation. We heartily concur with this view. MAP is designed *specifically* to show why the use of unemployment as a weapon against inflation should not even be *considered*.

MAP frees monetary and fiscal policy so that instead of using unemployment to fight inflation by *reducing* total money spending, total real spending can be *increased* to fight unemployment. MAP restrains total spending only after full employment has been attained when such restraint is necessary to avoid demand inflation.

As long as there is room for expansion in the economy, MAP will not hinder the increases in total spending that are essential for the increased employment and production of a healthy economy. Moreover, as the MAP disincentive reduces the rate of increase in prices, the previous rate of increase in *spending* will *buy* more products. Firms will then hire additional employees to produce more products and will invest in additional equipment. This increase in real production will provide some help for the unemployed, correcting the moral wrong of putting one group of individuals on the forefront of the fight against inflation.

Only when there is no room for any further expansion of output in response to increased *buying* would it become necessary to restrain further increases in total spending. Monetary or fiscal measures would then be required to reduce the increase in total spending to the level of the limited possible increase in output and employment.

This, of course, does not mean that when increases in total spending can no longer increase total output and employment, the government is powerless to affect the unemployment rate. There are many other ways to reduce unemployment. The government could invest in increasing labor skills, labor mobility, and employability or in improving the markets. But such programs would cost money, and with total spending in the economy, already at the maximum level possible without causing demand inflation, this would call for reductions in government spending elsewhere or for increases in taxes or for a tighter monetary policy to reduce *private* spending. The government must decide what actions to take regarding such proposals. If more is to be given to some and the total output cannot be expanded, something must be taken away from others. We believe that opportunities to increase total output in a free economy should be expanded as much as possible—but not more so.

Labor's third equity concern is that consumers be protected from "runaway price increases for the four necessities of life—food, energy, housing, and medical care." Although we agree that protection should be provided to the greatest degree possible, any anti-inflation proposal must take into account the realities of life. In the first place, a great part of the income spent on "the four necessities" goes for luxuries—and even flagrant waste. Only a minimum income deserves absolute protection, and no one can tell consumers what items are "necessary." Second, if there is a decrease in the real growth rate, or if a natural disaster destroys a large part of the food supply, or if a large increase occurs in import prices which the United States does not control, there will be less to go around for all. If any group is completely protected from all loss, then all the loss is concentrated on the remaining groups. In our personal view, only the very poor can validly claim special protection under the law because they cannot bear their "fair share" of an overall "belt tightening." But MAP does not guarantee anything in terms of real income. In effect, MAP tells us that there is exactly 100 percent to go around, and competition and individual and collective bargaining will continue to determine how it will be divided. Any other policy would be a violation and an abrogation of the normal competitive and bargaining procedures that form the basis of our economic system. If individual firms wish to grant their workers a certain specific guaranteed income, they are free to do so. But the government should guarantee only equality of opportunity, a job, and a minimum income to ensure freedom from extreme deprivation. Of course, all of this is subject to change in our established democratic system of government, and MAP does not try to usurp any of the system's sovereignty.

Both of us have strong inclinations to improve on the established division of the national income, but we have tried to keep them out of the present work. We realize that our preferences would not necessarily be shared by everyone who would like to bring about overall prosperity and price stability.

Labor's fourth equity concern is an insufficient exemption from the President's wage increase standard of low wage rates. We suspect that MAP will be criticized on the same grounds. MAP can be adjusted to favor low-wage workers, but it must be recognized that this can only be achieved at the expense of other incomes.

Much as we sympathize with the humane objectives of labor's concerns about the inequities in the government's program, we think that it is a serious mistake for labor to accept at face value the government's declaration that overcoming the current inflation requires hardship, sacrifice, or belt-tightening. This basic assumption is wrong. On the contrary, as long as we have millions of unemployed workers who are able and willing to work and a vast, unused productive capacity, we can *increase* our output and *raise* our standard of living. We do not have to tighten our belts. We can *loosen* them as soon as we give up our vain attempts to cure inflation by placing unemployment-creating restraints on total spending.

It is indeed an extraordinary idea that to stop inflation and to put our unemployed men and women and equipment to work, we must *reduce* our output, our consumption, and our investment. This strange belief seems to have resulted from a confusion between *sacrifice of real income,* which is not needed (rather, the reverse is true), and restraint of money income.

A *restraint* is not the same thing as a *sacrifice.* A restraint on one party *becomes* a sacrifice only if it is not accompanied by corresponding restraints by the remaining parties. That is why only a policy that completely integrates restraints on wage and price increases with reductions in increases in total spending can cure inflation. The benefit then is not only an end to the direct evils of the inflation, but also the possible expansion of employment, output, consumption, and investment for economic growth as the economy reaches its full productive potential.

MAP would mobilize the price and market mechanism for such a uniform and equitable application of the required restraints. No sacrifices would be necessary to reap the benefits except the sacrifice of a harmful tradition.

efficiency concerns

The second category of concerns expressed by labor falls under the criterion of efficiency. Labor's first efficiency concern is the fear that the government's program threatens to discontinue regulatory actions designed to protect workers from environmental and economic hazards. We heartily agree that such "economies" should not be part of an anti-inflation program. Regulatory questions should be decided on their own right and not on the basis of their inflationary impact. Efficiency is desirable even when there is no inflation. The fact that regulatory programs may raise costs and prices is not an appropriate criterion. *All* economic activities—private and public—involve costs. A regulatory activity should be undertaken if its social benefits outweigh its social costs; one that does not should not be instituted.

A second efficiency concern expressed in labor's anti-inflation statement is the need for flexibility in the program. Labor argues that wage controls are inflexible. MAP permits maximum flexibility in the system and leaves all wages and prices free to adjust to competition and free bargaining. What MAP does is only to require any real changes in preferences or in productive possibilities to be reflected in *relative* price changes rather than in changes in the absolute price level. By eliminating the *inflationary* element from each price change but leaving *relative* price changes intact, MAP provides the maximum amount of *useful* flexibility.

Labor's third efficiency concern is related to the foreign prices of the dollar or the reverse—the dollar prices of foreign currencies. The important effect of MAP on foreign exchange rates is that to the degree that domestic inflation is diminished, the dollar becomes a better store of value. Under MAP, more people, both foreigners and Americans, will want to hold dollars rather than other currencies, and the foreign prices of the dollar will rise. However, this is not properly a part of any anti-inflation program. If the value of the dollar rises, imports become cheaper but exporting becomes more difficult. If the dollar falls, American goods become more competitive. This increases the demand for American exports and reduces the domestic demand for imports, thereby increasing American employment. Labor, by blaming the government for both the decline in the value of the dollar and for our lagging exports (compared with our imports), seems to want to have it both ways. The issue of foreign exchange is far too often confused with the issue of inflation. We want to cure the inflation to stabilize the value of the dollar in buying goods and services *in this country*—not to stabilize the price of the dollar in terms of any foreign currency.

discrimination

Labor's position quite rightly reflects a concern about the government's intentions to punish anyone who disregards its guidelines. It is extremely dangerous to distort laws and employ them for purposes for which they were not intended. This could lead to a program of public scapegoating without due process, as well as to breakdowns in the economic system that would be far worse than anything that could result from inflation. MAP alleviates all of these problems. Anybody who chooses to is allowed to raise prices. The criteria of profitability and feasibility are left to the individuals concerned. MAP only provides the anti-inflation incentive to keep inflationary impacts and deflationary impacts exactly balanced, so that the desired low or zero rate of inflation is achieved.

The AFL–CIO's anti-inflation program ends by suggesting that even though the organization does not like controls, it prefers them to the available alternative courses of action. Such an embracing of the unacceptable is a reaction to the inefficiencies—and, even more, to the inequities—of the government program. We believe that if labor were to study MAP seriously, it would be saved from such a desperate step. By keeping the government from trying to take the place of the market, MAP provides all the benefits we have hoped to achieve from past and present controls and, at the same time, avoids all the manifold evils of controls. MAP applies the necessary anti-inflation incentives to *all* sources of income, treats *all* Americans equally, and provides a prompt and proper mechanism for the adjustment of inequities.

The AFL–CIO is totally correct in insisting that an anti-inflation program should not be arrived at piecemeal or in ill-designed stages. Americans deserve a complete, well-conceived, workable program with which to fight inflation. MAP provides the framework for such a program.

15

conclusion

By the 1930s, economists other than Keynes had abandoned the problem of unemployment, relinquishing it to the politicians. Their hands were clean. Unemployment was merely a political issue: unruly workers were unwilling to accept sufficiently low real wages to make it profitable for capitalists to produce. By viewing unemployment not as a political issue but as a technical issue, however, Keynes returned the problem of unemployment to economics. If unemployment were a technical problem, it should have a technical solution that could be designed into the economic system.

The technical solution that Keynes suggested—government regulation of the flow of total spending in the economy by adjusting the quantity of money and the government budget—was not easily introduced. Lerner gave it the name "functional finance." Challengers of Keynes' policy initially said that this functional finance undermined the basis of the capitalistic system. By the 1960s, however, it was generally accepted; instead of undermining the capitalistic system, economists began to view functional finance as the system's savior.

However, the Keynesian solution to unemployment had a technical flaw. It failed to maintain a constant price level.[1] It could produce and maintain full employment, but it could not prevent inflation. At first, severe inflationary consequences were avoided because there was an established belief in, or expectation of, a constant price level. But once this store of good will was exhausted and the government's guarantee of full employment was built into the system, the emergence of inflation undermined Keynes' solution to the unemployment problem. This led many economists to abandon not only the inflation problem but also the unemployment problem to the politicians. Keynesianism was pronounced dead.

The right wing was probably the first to claim victory. To these right-wing economists, Keynes was a modern-day John Law who had achieved a higher level of employment than could be sustained by the trickery of bestowing economic legitimacy on easy-money policies. Inflation was the inevitable penalty.

The left wing also claimed victory, suggesting that the Keynesian solu-

---

[1] For further discussion, see Lerner, "From Pre-Keynes to Post-Keynes" (1977).

tion was merely a stop-gap measure designed to hold the capitalistic system together in the face of an irrepressible class struggle over profits and wages. That solution had worked temporarily, but the inherent contradictions of capitalism expressed themselves in inflation.

The similarity of these two political views is striking. The only difference is in the nature of the outcome. One considers the capitalistic system to be basically stable as long as the government doesn't meddle in it. The other views the system as basically unstable, whatever the government does.

MAP is in direct juxtaposition to both views. It offers a technical solution to the problem of inflation, just as Keynes offered a technical solution to the problem of unemployment. In our view, Keynes' solution was a real solution with a technical fault. It did not rely on illusion. But it was a solution to unemployment—not a solution to inflation (which no one ever claimed it was). MAP does provide a solution to inflation. In conjunction with functional finance, MAP restores the issues of both unemployment and inflation to economics.

MAP is not only for the moderate; both the left and the right can support it. If the left is correct and there is an immutable class struggle over the distribution of income—either between profits and wages or between various types of wages—MAP, by laying bare the realities of that struggle, will actually hasten the end of capitalism that the illusions of inflation might otherwise delay for a few years. If the right is correct, MAP will provide the monetary stability necessary for the system to function by not permitting the government to gain from the windfalls of inflation. Thus, if the right is correct, MAP will prevent government from even temporarily increasing employment by inflationary illusion.

However, if we are correct in viewing inflation as merely a technical problem, MAP—in conjunction with functional finance—will provide a method of achieving the goals of both price stability and full employment. MAP, if implemented, will provide a perfect test of the competing theories.

To succeed, MAP requires that government be committed to ending inflation and be capable of enforcing the property rights that MAP embodies. Government commitment is necessary because the effectiveness of MAP is primarily contingent on the public's expectation that inflation will be stopped. If individuals are unsure of the government's resolve to end inflation and believe that monetary regulators will either continue to try to expand the economy above a sustainable level or quickly dismantle MAP, firms will expect prices to rise more rapidly than ever once MAP is eliminated. In this case, the introduction of MAP may cause shortages as sellers hold back their supplies in anticipation of the higher prices they expect to receive after MAP has been buried.

These shortages will be limited, however, and the sellers will soon discover that the inflation has stopped. Their expectations of rising prices will then weaken, and the air will pour out of the expectational inflation balloon. Thus, MAP will eliminate expectations of inflation by eliminating the inflation. As expectations that it will be necessary to raise prices decrease, the price of

MAP Credit will also decrease. And the expectation that MAP will meet its demise will also fade away.

The government's ability to enforce MAP is the second essential requirement for the success of the plan. If any law is to be enforceable, it cannot be imposed on an unwilling public. Unless a law is generally accepted as fair, it will soon fail. This is why we so carefully considered the neutrality of MAP.

Some economists have objected to this neutrality because MAP does not directly control labor unions. They argue that MAP will fail because it will permit labor unions to make demands that will bankrupt firms. We doubt that this will prove true, at least in the United States.

In our view, one of the most hopeful signs during past attempts to institute incomes policies has been labor's reasonableness and cooperative spirit, even when inequities between wages and prices became apparent. By and large, labor met the government's wage guidelines until it became apparent that business was not meeting the price guidelines. We believe that labor does desire a successful anti-inflation policy.

MAP is neither a conservative nor a liberal policy. It is a synthesis of both. MAP incorporates the conservative's fear of bureaucracy and preference for the market with the liberal's belief in the need for a fair incomes policy. It is a policy that should receive broad, bipartisan support.

There is, of course, the question of whether we really want to stop the inflation. Contrary to many accounts in the press, inflation does not hurt everyone; some people benefit from inflation and some lose. Inflation has its own constituency, which will be hurt if inflation is stopped. This includes those who currently benefit from short-run rigidities in the system and those who have placed their bets on inflation continuing. The counterparts of these groups are hurt by inflation. The political determination of whether or not to stop the inflation depends in large part on the relative strengths of these groups.

We believe the ultimate decision will be to stop the inflation. To fail to stop the inflation would (1) undermine the stability of the national currency, (2) significantly increase the cost of conducting business, and (3) destroy our monetary system. At some point, these damages to society as a whole, combined with the interests of the losing faction, must overcome the preferences of those who gain from inflation. This is why historically all severe inflations have been stopped.

To argue that inflation will ultimately be ended does not mean that it will be ended by MAP—at least not immediately. Despite our inherent optimism, we recognize that this book does not answer all the questions. Even though the reader may have reached the "it can be done" phase, he or she will probably still be highly skeptical—and rightly so.

Before any new program is implemented, it should be thoroughly discussed and analyzed so that as many loopholes as possible can be found and corrected. Alternative courses of action should be carefully compared to enable the intricate political foundations to be built. The theoretically convincing must be translated into the politically acceptable.

The initial novelty of MAP will delay its acceptance. At some point, however, a new approach to inflation must be tried. Novelty cannot continue to be a disqualification when all other proposals have failed. It is true that plans invariably sound better on paper than they do when they are applied. It is only natural to expect the worst. According to Murphy's Law, "If anything can go wrong, it will." But such considerations cannot indefinitely preclude action.

The question is whether government can be made to accept the reasonableness of the market and business can be convinced to forsake its "old-time religion," or whether MAP will remain a far-off dream. Given the realities, the world will probably remain MAPless for some time to come.

In place of MAP, the government is much more likely to follow one of three policies:

(1)   The "eclectic" approach (a little of this and a little of that).
(2)   Ever-tightening monetary and fiscal policies.
(3)   Wage and price controls.

To us, this prospect is discouraging, but not disheartening. The first of these policies ultimately leads to the second, the second leads to the third, and the third leads to MAP.

The "eclectic" approach has been followed for about 30 years, and we expect this course of inaction to continue for a while longer. It has always failed in the past, and it will always fail in the future. This is becoming generally recognized, and the political mood of the country now seems to be swinging toward the second policy. Keynesian economics is being forsaken, and the government is beginning to tighten monetary and fiscal policy—whatever the consequences.

We estimate that this belt-tightening will persist for two or three more years, but such policies will not produce the desired effects. The tightened money supply will have only a small effect, if any, on reducing the inflation and a rather large effect on reducing real economic output and employment. Initially, these effects will probably be attributed to unexpected changes in the velocity of money and "acts of God." But in the end, we do not feel that people will accept the high level of unemployment that is required for this approach to succeed. It will then become apparent that monetary policy alone is not an effective tool against inflation. This does not mean that monetary policy alone *cannot* work; it means that the political realities will not *let* it work. As unemployment increases, shortfalls in tax revenues and automatic countercyclical programs will increase the deficit, while additional new demands for defense and special unemployment assistance programs will make the role of monetary policy more and more difficult. At some point, the political resolve will fail and politicians facing difficult elections ahead will again decide to support controls so that their opponents should not be able to outpromise them. We will then move on to the third policy—regulatory wage and price controls.

Like past attempts at regulatory restraints, these attempts will once more fail. Wage and price controls are simply incompatible with a free market economy. Either the controls or the market must prevail.

But even if continuous regulatory control is eventually established, MAP will ultimately be arrived at as the controls are adjusted to make them more flexible and efficient. Guidelines for allowable prices will increasingly be made to reflect the normal cost—the outlay on the additional inputs required—which closely resembles the free MAP Credit granted to firms that hire or acquire additional productive inputs. Attempts to introduce flexibility into the controls will be instituted in much the same way that earlier forms of commodity rationing were improved and rationalized. The permanent controls will become more and more MAP-like. Finally, MAP will be arrived at.

We will close with a parable. The local, noble tyrant of a Russian village gave a man who had displeased him a choice of three punishments—eat a dish of stinking fish, receive 40 lashes, or pay the enormous fine of 1,000 rubles. Initially, the man chose the fish. But after eating half of the dish, he could not keep any more down, so he chose the 40 lashes. But after 30 lashes, he could bear no more, so he finally agreed to pay the 1,000 rubles.

As the story implies, there is a better way.

bibliography

American Enterprise Institute. *Real Wage Insurance.* Washington, D.C., 1979.

Bailey, Martin. "Moderation of Inflation by Recession and Control." *Brookings Papers on Economic Activity,* Vol. 3, The Brookings Institution, 1976, pp. 585–633.
Ball, R.J., and Doyle, Peter, ed. *Inflation.* Middlesex, England: Penguin Books, 1969.
Bellan, Reuben. "An Alternative Strategy against Cost Push Inflation." *Middlebury Conference on Anti-Inflation Policy: Proceedings,* forthcoming.
Boyer, Andre. "La Serisette: Un Impot Francais au Coeur des Formation des Pris." *Public Finance,* Vol. XXX, No. 3 (1975), pp. 452–67.
Bronfenbrenner, Martin and Holzman, Franklyn D. "Survey of Inflation Theory." *American Economic Review,* Vol. 53, No. 4 (September 1963), pp. 593–661.
Brunner, Karl, ed. *Proceedings of the Conference on Wage and Price Controls at Rochester University.* New York, October 1973.

Cagan, Phillip. *The Hydra-Headed Monster.* Washington, D.C.: American Enterprise Institute, 1974.
Clegg, Hugh. *How to Run an Incomes Policy, and Why We Made Such A Mess of The Last One.* London: Heinemann, 1971.
Colander, David. "Tax and Market Based Incomes Policies: The Interface between Theory and Practice." *Middlebury Conference on Anti-Inflation Policy: Proceedings,* forthcoming.
Colander, David. *Incentive Based Incomes Policies.* Joint Economic Committee Print, forthcoming.
Colander, David. "Incomes Policies: MIP, WIPP and TIP." *Journal of Post Keynesian Economics,* Spring 1979(a), pp. 91–100.
Colander, David. "A Value Added TIP" in Colander, *Solutions To Inflation.* New York: Harcourt Brace Jovanovich, 1979(b), pp. 188–92.
Colander, David, ed. *Solutions To Inflation.* New York: Harcourt Brace Jovanovich, 1979(c).
Colander, D.C. "Rationality, Expectations and Functional Finance" in Gapinski and Rockwell, ed., *Essays in Post-Keynesian Economics.* Cambridge, Massachusetts: Ballinger Press, 1979(d).
Colander, D.C., and Koford, K. "Realytic and Analytic Syntheses of Macro- and Microeconomics." *Journal of Economic Issues,* Vol. XIII, September 1979, pp. 707–31.
Colm, Gerhard. "On the Road to Economic Stabilization." *Social Research,* Vol. 15, September 1948, pp. 265–76.

Dildine, L., and Sunley, E. "Administrative Problems of Tax-Based Incomes Policies." *Brookings Papers on Economic Activity,* Vol. 2, The Brookings Institution, 1978, pp. 363–89.

Fellner, W. *Towards a Reconstruction of Macroeconomics.* Washington, D.C.: American Enterprise Institute, 1976.
Flemming, John. *Inflation.* Oxford, England: Oxford University Press, 1978.
Fogarty, M.P. "Fiscal Measure and Wage Settlements." *British Journal of Industrial Relations,* Vol. 11, 1973, pp. 29–65.

120

Fogarty, M.P. *We Can Stop Rising Prices.* Dublin: Economic and Social Research Institute, March 1970.

Friedman, Milton. "The Role of Monetary Policy." *American Economic Review,* Vol. 58 (1), 1968, pp. 1–17.

Friedman, Milton. "Using Escalators to Fight Inflation." *Fortune,* Vol. 90, July 1974, pp. 94–97, 174–76.

Friedman, Milton; Giersch, Herbert; Bernstein, Edward M.; Fellner, William; and Kafka, Alexandre. *Essays on Inflation and Indexation.* Washington, D.C.: American Enterprise Institute, 1974.

Gapinski, J., and Rockwell, C. *Essays in Post-Keynesian Inflation.* Cambridge, Massachusetts; Ballinger Press, 1979.

Goodwin, Craufurd D., ed. *Exhortation and Controls.* Washington, D.C.: The Brookings Institution, 1975.

Grayson, Jackson C. *Confessions of a Price Controller.* Homewood, Illinois: Dow Jones-Irwin, 1974.

Howard, J.V. "A Method of Controlling Inflation." *Economic Journal,* Vol. 86, December 1976, pp. 832–44.

Isard, Peter. "The Effectiveness of Using the Tax System to Curb Inflationary Collective Bargains: An Analysis of the Wallich–Weintraub Plan." *Journal of Political Economy,* Vol. 81, 1973, pp. 729–40.

Jevons, W.S. *Money and the Mechanism of Exchange.* London: Kegan Paul, 1875.

Keynes, J.M. *The General Theory* (1936), First Harbinger Edition. New York: Harcourt Brace Jovanovich, 1964.

Klein, Benjamin. "The Competitive Supply of Money." *Journal of Money, Credit and Banking,* Vol. VI, November 1975, pp. 423–53.

Korliras, Panayotis G., and Thorn, Richard, ed. *Modern Macroeconomics.* New York: Harper and Row, 1979.

Kosters, Marvin H. *Controls and Inflation.* Washington, D.C.: The American Enterprise Institute, 1975.

Kotowitz, Yehamda, and Portes, Richard. "A Tax on Wage Increases: A Theoretical Analysis." *Journal of Public Economics,* 3, 1974, pp. 113–32.

Krauss, Lawrence B., and Salant, Walter S., ed. *Worldwide Inflation.* Washington, D.C.: The Brookings Institution, 1977.

Lancaster, K. "Productivity Geared Wages Policy." *Economica,* New Series 25, August 1958, pp. 199–212.

Lanzillotti, Robert; Roberts, Blaine; and Hamilton, Mary. *Phase II in Review: The Price Commission Experience.* Washington, D.C.: The Brookings Institution, 1975.

Latham, R.W., and Peel D.A. "The Tax on Wage Increases When the Firm Is a Monopsonist." *Journal of Public Economics* 8, 1977, pp. 247–53.

Lerner, Abba. *Economics of Employment.* New York: McGraw-Hill, 1951.

Lerner, Abba. *Flation.* New York: Quadrangle Books, 1972.

Lerner, Abba. "Stagflation." *Intermountain Economic Review,* Fall 1975, pp. 1–7.

Lerner, Abba. "A Reluctant Keynesian." *Intermountain Economic Review,* Fall 1976, pp. 55–60.

Lerner, Abba. "From Pre-Keynes to Post-Keynes." *Social Research,* Vol. 44, Autumn 1977, pp. 387–415.

Lerner, Abba. "Stagflation—Its Cause and Cure." *Challenge,* Vol. 20, September/October 1977, pp. 14–19.

Lerner, Abba. "A Wage Increase Permit Plan to Stop Inflation." *Brookings Papers on Economic Activity,* Vol. 2, The Brookings Institution, 1978, pp. 491–505.

Lerner, Abba. "A Mutation in the Aggregate Price and Employment Equilibrating Mechanism of a Market Economy." *Tel Aviv Conference on Development in an Inflationary World: June 16–19, 1979 Proceedings,* forthcoming.

Lerner, Abba. "The Market Anti-Inflation Plan" in Gapinski and Rockwell, *Essays in Post-Keynesian Inflation.* Cambridge, Massachusetts: Ballinger Press, 1979, pp. 217–29.

Lerner, Abba. "MAP: The Market Mechanism Cure for Stagflation." *Atlantic Economic Review,* Vol. 7, No. 1 (March 1979), pp. 12–19.

Lerner, Abba, and Colander, David. "MAP, A Cure for Inflation" in Colander, *Solutions to Inflation.* New York: Harcourt Brace Jovanovich, 1979.

Mayer, Thomas. "Innovative Incomes Policies, A Skeptic's View." *Middlebury Conference on Anti-Inflation Policy: Proceedings,* forthcoming.

Mayer, Thomas. *The Structure of Monetarism.* New York: W.W. Norton and Co., 1978.

Meade, J.E. *Wages and Prices in a Mixed Economy.* Institute of Economic Affairs, Occasional Paper 35, 1971.

Mill, John Stuart. *Principles of Political Economy* (1848), W.J. Ashley, ed. London: Longmans, Green and Co., 1921.

Moore, Thomas Gale. *U.S. Incomes Policy, Its Rationale and Development.* Washington, D.C.: American Enterprise Institute, 1971.

Nordhaus, William. "Tax-Based Incomes Policies: A Better Mousetrap." *Middlebury Conference on Anti-Inflation Policy,* forthcoming.

Okun, A. Statement before the Committee on Banking, Housing, and Urban Affairs, U.S. Senate, May 22, 1978, reprinted in Colander, *Solutions to Inflation,* pp. 176–82.

Okun, A. "Inflation: Its Mechanics and Welfare Costs." *Brookings Papers on Economic Activity,* Vol. 2, The Brookings Institution, 1975, pp. 351–90.

Okun, A. "The Great Stagflation Swamp." *Challenge,* November/December 1977, pp. 6–13.

Okun, A., and Perry, G., ed. "Innovative Policies To Slow Inflation." *Brookings Papers on Economic Activity,* Vol. 2, The Brookings Institution, 1978.

Parkin, Michael, and Summer, Michael, ed. *Incomes Policy and Inflation.* Manchester: Manchester University Press, 1974.

Parkin, Michael, and Zis, George, ed. *Inflation in The World Economy.* Manchester: Manchester University Press, 1976.

Pigou, A.C. "Empty Economic Boxes: A Reply." *Economic Journal,* December 1922, pp. 458–65.

Portes, Richard. "Economic Reforms in Hungary." *American Economic Review,* Vol. 60, 1970, pp. 307–13.

Portes, R.D. "Hungary, the Experience of Market Socialism." *ODEPLAN/IDS Roundtable,* Santiago, Chile, March–April 1972.

Rees, Albert. "New Policies to Fight Inflation: Sources of Skepticism." *Brookings Papers on Economic Activity,* Vol. 2, The Brookings Institution, 1978, pp. 453–90.

Scott, M.F.G. "A Tax on Price Increases." *Economic Journal,* Vol. 71, June 1961, pp. 350–66.

Seidman, Larry. "A New Approach to the Control of Inflation." *Challenge,* Vol. 19, July/August 1976(a), pp. 39–43.

Seidman, Larry. "Would Tax-Shifting Undermine The Tax-Based Incomes Policy?" *Journal of Economic Issues,* Vol. 12, September 1978, pp. 647–76.

Seidman, Larry. "The Role of a Tax-Based Incomes Policy." *American Economic Review: Papers and Proceedings,* Vol. 69, No. 2 (May 1979), pp. 202–206.

Seidman, Larry. "A Payroll Tax-Credit to Restrain Inflation." *National Tax Journal,* Vol. XXIX, December 1976(b), pp. 398–412.

Sheahan, John. *The Wage Price Guideposts.* Washington, D.C.: The Brookings Institution, 1967.

Sheahan, John. "Incomes Policies in an Open Economy: Domestic and External Interactions." *Middlebury Conference on Anti-Inflation Policy: Proceedings,* forthcoming.

Slitor, Richard. "Tax Based Incomes Policy: Technical and Administrative." Report prepared for the Board of Governors of the Federal Reserve System, March 20, 1978.

Stein, Herbert. "Price-Fixing as Seen by a Price Fixer, Part II." *Contemporary Economic Problems 1978,* W. Fellner, ed. Washington, D.C.: American Enterprise Institute, 1978.

Strebel, Paul. "Value Added Policy: A Supplement to Deflationary Demand Management." *Public Finance,* Vol. 33, No. 1–2 (1978), pp. 135–47.

Streeten, Paul. "Wages, Prices and Productivity." *Kyklos,* Vol. 15, 1962, reprinted in R. Ball and P. Doyle, *Inflation,* Penguin Books, 1969.

Summer, M.T. "Le Prelevement Conjoncturel." *Public Finance,* Vol. 30, No. 3 (1975), pp. 461–67.

Trevithick, J.A. *Inflation.* Middlesex, England: Penguin Books, 1977.

Trevithick, J.A., and Malvey, C. *The Economics of Inflation.* London: Martin Robertson, 1975.

Ture, Norman. "Tax-Based Incomes Policy: Pain or Pleasure in Pursuit of Price-Level Stability." *Tax Foundations Tax Review,* Vol. XXXIX, No. 6 (June 1978), 23–30.

Ulman, Lloyd, and Flanagan, Robert. *Wage Restraint: A Study of Incomes Policies in Western Europe.* Berkeley, California: University of California Press, 1971.

U.S. Government. *Real Wage Insurance: Hearings before the Committee on Ways and Means,* January 29, 30, 31, February 1, 2, 5, 1979. Washington, D.C.: U.S. Government Printing Office, 1979.

U.S. Government, Council on Wage and Price Stability. *Fact Book: Wage and Price Standards.* Washington, D.C.: U.S. Government Printing Office, October 31, 1979.

von Hayek, F.A. *Denationalization of Money.* Hobart Paper 70, 1976.

von Hayek, F.A. "The Use of Knowledge in Society." *American Economic Review,* Vol. XXXV, No. 4 (September 1945), pp. 519–30.

von Weitzäcker, Carl Christian. "Political Limits of Traditional Stabilization Policy." Mimeo, May 1975.

Walker, Michael, ed. *The Illusion of Wage and Price Control*. Vancouver, Canada: The Fraser Institute, 1976.

Wallich, Henry C. "Phase II and the Proposal for a Tax Oriented Income Policy." *Review of Social Economy,* Vol. 30, March 1972, pp. 1–13.

Wallich, Henry C. "The 1970 Mid-Year Review of the State of the Economy." Hearings before the Joint Economic Committee, 91st Congress, Second Session, Pt. 3(a).

Wallich, Henry, and Weintraub, Sidney. "Tax Based Incomes Policies." *Journal of Economic Issues,* Vol. 5, June 1971, pp. 1–17.

Weber, Arnold. *In Pursuit of Price Stability: The Wage Price Freeze of 1971.* Washington, D.C.: The Brookings Institution, 1973.

Weintraub, Sidney. *Capitalism's Inflation and Unemployment Crisis*. Reading, Massachusetts: Addison-Wesley Publishing Co., 1978.

Weintraub, Sidney. "TIPS Against Inflation." *Middlebury Conference on Anti-Inflation Policy: Proceedings,* forthcoming.

Weintraub, Sidney. "The Incomes Policy in the Monetarist Programme." *The Bankers Magazine,* August 1970, pp. 71–73.

Weintraub, Sidney. "A Feasible Anti-Inflation Incomes Policy." *Lloyds Bank Review,* Vol. 99, January 1971, pp. 1–12. Also found in the Congressional Record, November 20, 1970, E9783.

Weintraub, Sidney. "Incomes Policy: Completing The Stabilization Triangle." *Journal of Economic Issues,* Vol. 6, December 1972, pp. 105–22.

Weintraub, Sidney. *TIP: To Stop Stagflation*. Bryn Mawr, Pennsylvania: 1978 Frank M. Engle Lecture of The American College.

Wood, Adrian. *A Theory of Pay*. Cambridge, England: Cambridge University Press, 1978.

index

a

AFL–CIO, 107
Anti-inflation accounting credit. *See*
    MAP Credit
Anti-inflation incentive, 13, 97. *See also*
    Counter-inflationary disincentive
Anti-inflation policies, 14–31

b

Bailey, Martin, 85
Bellan, Reuben, 85
Black markets, 22–23, 25
Business' anti-inflation plan, 100–103
    criticism of, 103–106
    and productivity, 105–106

c

Capital inputs, adjustments for, 56–57
Capital investment, 40
Circular causation, 18–19
Colander, David, 31, 64 n
Colm, Gerhard, 27
Controls, 26
Cost push, 70
Counter-inflationary disincentive, 4–6,
    29, 34–35
    in MAP, 13, 37, 43, 110
    See also MAP Credit
Credit money, 14–16

d

Deficits, 9–10, 64–66, 88–89, 90–93
    and inflation, 64–66, 91
Deflation, expectational, 5
Dildine, L., 78
Direct relativity bargaining, 85–86

e

Expectational deflation, 5, 79
Expectational inflation, 32, 33, 62, 90

f

Federal Reserve (FED), 50, 65–66, 67,
    68, 105
Fiscal policy, 68, 104–106, 111
Flaw in our economic system, 3,
    19–20, 29–30
"Free market in money" proposals,
    84–85
Friedman, Milton, 6
Full employment, 32–33
    high and low, 71
Functional finance, 1–2, 17, 19, 26,
    36–38, 64–66, 76–77,
    104–105, 115–16
    and its technical flaw, 115, 116
Functional and nonfunctional changes,
    4, 64–66, 75–76, 105–106,
    115–16
Functions of price, and of markets,
    29–30, 30 n

g

Gold receipts, 15
Government deficits, 64–66
    and business anti-inflation plan,
    103–105
Government as victim of inflation,
    90–91
Government's anti-inflation plan,
    87–90, 92–95
    and compliance "ad-hoc-ery,"
    96–97
    criticism of, 89–91, 95–99
    and MAP, 97

125

A 0
B 1
C 2
D 3
E 4
F 5
G 6
H 7
I 8
J 9